**Connecting Speaking & Writing
in Second Language Writing Instruction**

Michigan Series on Teaching Multilingual Writers

Series Editors
Diane Belcher (Georgia State University) and
Jun Liu (University of Arizona)

Connecting Speaking & Writing in Second Language Writing Instruction

Robert Weissberg

 Michigan Series on Teaching Multilingual Writers

Ann Arbor
THE UNIVERSITY OF MICHIGAN PRESS

⊗ Printed on acid-free paper

2009   2008   2007   2006   4   3   2   1

Library of Congress Cataloging-in-Publication Data

Weissberg, Robert.
      Connecting speaking & writing in second language writing instruction / Robert Weissberg.
          p.   cm.—(Michigan series on teaching multilingual writers)
      Includes bibliographical references and indexes.
      ISBN-13: 978-0-472-03032-3 (pbk. : alk. paper)
      ISBN-10: 0-472-03032-9 (pbk. : alk. paper)
          1. Composition (Language arts) 2. Second language acquisition. I. Title. II. Title:
      Connecting speaking and writing in second language writing instruction. III. Series.

      P53.27.W45   2006
      808'.042071—dc22   2006044582

For Bernie and Milagro

Acknowledgments

I want to express my thanks to the friends and colleagues who have helped me in so many ways to bring this project to completion. They are, in no particular order, Tony Silva, Paul Matsuda, Walter Zakahi, Rosalinda Barrera, Beth Hewett, Sondra Perl, Anne Hubbell, Terese Thonus, Ann Michaels, Robert Heiser, Tara Gray, and the members of my faculty writers' group at New Mexico State University: Bob Blaire, Alison Newby, and Mardy Mahaffy, among many others.

A special thanks goes to my series editors Diane Belcher and Jun Liu, and my editor at the University of Michigan Press, Kelly Sippell, for their patience and faith in this project. And finally to the multitude of second language students in my classes, whose interaction with me, oral and written, has taught me more than I can estimate about writing.

Grateful acknowledgment is made to the following authors, publishers, and individuals for permission to reprint previously published materials.

Copyright Clearance Center for Teachers College Press for excerpt of classroom dialogue published in *Opening Dialog: Understanding the Dynamics of Language and Learning in the English Classroom* by Martin Nystrand. Copyright © 1997.

Elsevier for excerpt from "Developmental relationships in the acquisition of English syntax: Writing vs. speech" by Robert Weissberg in *Learning and Instruction 10* (2000), p. 49. Reprinted with permission.

Elsevier for excerpt from "Speaking of writing: Some functions of talk in the ESL composition class" by Robert

Weissberg in *Journal of Second Language Writing, 3* (1994), p. 137. Reprinted with permission.

Journal of Basic Writing. Copyright 2002, the City University of New York. Reprinted from Volume 21, Number 2, by permission.

Students who allowed their work to be included in this book.

Every effort has been made to contact the copyright holders for permission to reprint borrowed material. We regret any oversights that may have occurred and will rectify them in future printings of this book.

Contents

Series Foreword

While the reading-writing connection may have been some-what neglected of late (see Hirvela, 2004), the speaking-writing connection in both first and second language (L1, L2) circles has been ignored to a much greater degree. In L2 writing, the limited attention to the possible pedagogical value of the con-nectedness of oral and written discourse may be due to our eagerness to promote L2 writing as a legitimate field of study and practice in its own right, out from under the shadow of spo-ken language traditionally cast upon it by linguists interested in second language acquisition (SLA) (see Matsuda, 2001). But the separation of writing from speaking in L2 classrooms, as well as in L1 school settings, may also be the legacy of a respected body of research on the distance between orality and literacy (e.g., Halliday, 1989), as Hyland (2002) has pointed out. Hyland has argued that the distancing of speaking from writing, both theoretically and pedagogically, may actually be more harmful than helpful, as "the effectiveness of a written text does not depend on removing readers [interlocutors] from it, but on correctly identifying an audience and employing the communicative conventions to which they are most likely to respond" (p. 52).

Readers of Robert Weissberg's contribution to our series will find in it a compelling argument for rethinking and, indeed, reclaiming the speaking-writing connection in L2 classrooms resonating with the case Hyland makes and going far beyond it. Weissberg reminds us that much SLA research points to the crucial role that genuine, meaningful communication—i.e., social interaction—plays in all language learning, including literacy. Weissberg also brings to the attention of L2 writing specialists the compelling arguments of Vygotsky and other sociocultural theorists, whose work has not generally been well represented in the L2 writing literature but has been extremely influential in L1 literacy theory. What socioculturalists and other similar language theorists, such as Bakhtin, have to contribute, Weissberg notes, is insight into the foundational role that social interaction and resulting internalized talk, or inner speech, play in the development of the complex cognitive skills that we refer to as *writing*.

Weissberg, however, does much more than build arguments for linking speaking and writing in the L2 classroom. His book moves swiftly from theory to practice: showing us how developing concurrent oral-writing proficiencies can affect actual individual L2 learners, and telling us how synergistic dialogue-writing relationships can be fostered through writing tasks, group activities, conferencing, dialogue journals, and even teacher-written feedback. As an EAP (English for Academic Purposes) researcher who has extensively investigated speaking-writing relationships and a former director of an Intensive English Program, as well as a teacher of ESL students and TESOL teacher-trainees, Weissberg is able to offer the reader a richly theoretical and research-informed perspective on classroom practice in accessible prose, replete with vivid examples likely to be engaging for both pre- and in-service TESOL professionals. It seems highly probable that many readers of this book will be inspired to "socialize" their L2 composition classrooms and connect speaking and writing in ways they may have never before considered.

References

Halliday, M. A. K. (1989). *Spoken and written language*. Oxford: Oxford University Press.

Hirvela, A. (2004). *Connecting reading and writing in second language writing instruction*. Ann Arbor: University of Michigan Press.

Hyland, K. (2002). *Teaching and researching writing*. Harlow, UK: Longman/Pearson Education.

Matsuda, P. (2001). Reexamining audiolingualism: On the genesis of read-ing and writing in L2 studies. In D. Belcher & A. Hirvela (Eds.), *Linking literacies: Perspectives on L2 reading-writing connections* (pp. 84–108). Ann Arbor: University of Michigan Press.

Diane Belcher
Georgia State University

Jun Liu
Arizona State University

Chapter 1

An Introduction to Dialogue and Second Language Writing

"In the beginning is dialog."
(Roger Shuy, 1987, p. 891)

"Talk is the sea upon which all else floats."
(James Britton, 1970)

The most effective writing classrooms are not always quiet places. Certainly, students may at times be engrossed in individual writing tasks, but at other times the writing class might be mistaken for another kind of classroom altogether. Students may be actively engaged with each other and with their instructor—voices murmuring in conversation, occasionally punctuated with excitement, frustration, or even anger. Or students may be seated in small groups engaged in a joint project, working in pairs on a task, or carrying on a discussion as a whole class with individuals bidding for the instructor's attention. On other occasions, a student may take over the teacher's normal role to make an informal presentation from the front of the class. At these times one might mistake the writing classroom for a conversation course, a public speaking class, or a lecture-discussion class in an academic content area.

What does all this hubbub have to do with writing and, more specifically, with non-native speakers learning to write in their new language? After all, writing, like reading, is an individual, highly demanding cognitive activity requiring the writer's full attention and concentration. How then does a class that looks and sounds like a social gathering serve as the setting for the development of second language literacy?

This book addresses these questions. It looks at the ways that oral and written language interact for second language (L2) learners, and it describes a general approach to teaching L2 writing that is rooted in **dialogue**—dialogue between students and teacher, between student and tutor, among students, and in the minds of individual student writers (Ellis, 1999; Shuy, 1987). The main arguments to be made here are that writing, although it is most frequently accomplished by individuals working on their own, is a fundamentally social phenomenon and that it can best be acquired by L2 learners when it is embedded in the dialogue of social interaction—that is, when it floats on a sea of talk, to paraphrase James Britton (1970). Certainly, teachers can deal with their L2 students as individual, solitary writers, and there are times in most writing courses when it is necessary to do that. However, teachers also have the option to create within their classrooms a community of writers who, through dialogue, serve each other as tutors, coauthors, sounding boards, and critical readers.

If scholars in the area of L2 writing have tended to neglect the influence of oral language on the development of literacy, it may be a reaction to the short shrift historically given to writing by researchers in second language acquisition (SLA) and applied linguistics in general (Harklau, 2002). This book takes a wider view. It sees the written and oral modalities as inextricably linked developmentally for many learners, and social interaction as a powerful impetus in becoming biliterate.

Four Assumptions

The social context we will examine most closely (though not the only one we will consider) is the writing classroom itself. The argument for using a dialogue approach to teaching L2 writers rests on assumptions similar to those that underlie *communicative language teaching,* the movement that has revolutionized foreign and L2 teaching over the last 30 years (Nunan, 1999). It also owes much to more recent interactionist and sociocultural theories of SLA (Ellis, 1999; Hall & Verplaetse, 2000; Hall, Vitanova, & Marchenkova, 2005; Lantolf, 2000). The key assumptions are that:

1. The most effective language lessons are those that are genuinely communicative, meaningful, and relevant to learners.
2. Communicative language use involves people working together to exchange information, negotiate meaning, and accomplish tasks.
3. Classroom language learning is by nature a social enterprise. Thus, interaction is not just a precursor to, or a condition for, language learning—it is in itself a way of learning language.
4. Social interaction provides an ideal context for mastering complex cognitive skills like writing.

Although the first assumption is usually associated with the communicative approach to teaching oral language, it is also valid when applied to acquiring L2 literacy skills. Take the prescription to make lessons "meaningful," for example; a meaningful speech event implies at least two active interlocutors with something important to talk about. In the same way, a communicative approach to writing implies an interactive, cooperative relationship between the writer and his or her reader. It is by being conscious of their readers that good writers are able to construct texts that anticipate their readers' information needs and possible reactions. Thus, one important benefit of bringing dialogue into the writing class is to help L2 writers develop a strong *sense of audience.*

The second assumption calls for the use of pair and small group tasks in the writing classroom. In oral language classes, small group activities provide learners with the opportunity to negotiate meaning with each other through conversation. In the writing classroom, brainstorming and revision groups and one-on-one tutoring help writers to generate and clarify their ideas and to critique their own texts. In dialoging with their teachers and fellow students in class and with tutors in the writing center, apprentice writers learn to recognize the logical gaps, ambiguous references, and fuzzy statements hiding in their texts and how to mend them. They learn, in essence, to make sense on paper. Thus, a second benefit of creating a dialogic environment in the writing class is that it makes available to L2 students alternative strategies for *inventing and revising* the idea content of their writing and for developing written *coherence.*

The third assumption, that classroom language learning is inherently social, implies that injecting dialogue into the writing class is more than a means of livening up the occasional lesson by letting students work together while the teacher enjoys a well-deserved rest. The teacher is an important actor in the social dialogue of the classroom and has an important role to play at all times, not just during whole-group instruction, as will be discussed in greater detail in Chapter 4. But more important, the third assumption implies that dialogue is itself a general approach to teaching and learning to write in a second language. As such, it can inform all of our instructional decisions—from the ways we introduce our students to unfamiliar written genres, to the way we mark their papers. Thus, a third benefit of the dialogic approach is that it gives us a *consistent basis* for planning and executing writing lessons and for dealing with L2 writers and their texts.

The last assumption captures the notion that social communication is the bedrock on which an individual's literacy skills develop. This is the theoretical basis that underlies much of the discussion in the rest of this book and that will be examined in detail in Chapter 2. It is embodied in the quotation from James Britton (1970) with which this introductory chapter began and that informs Donald Rubin's (1988) extension of Britton's analogy when he makes a case for talk as a key element in learning to be literate: "We internalize talk, and it becomes thought. We externalize talk, and it becomes our link to social reality. We elaborate talk, and it becomes our bridge to literacy" (p. 3).

As will be shown in Chapter 2, Rubin's claims closely parallel the argument that Lev Vygotsky (1986) and the sociocultural theorists have made to explain the development of L1 literacy in children (Wells, 2000). A similar argument will be made for L2 writers of all ages.

Taken together, these four assumptions suggest that making interactive dialogue a regular feature of the writing classroom is a logical and natural extension of communicative language teaching.

The Plan of This Book

In arguing for a dialogic approach to teaching L2 writers, this book intends to accomplish two goals—first, to provide readers with a theoretical perspective on the importance of talk in L2 learners' development of written language; and second, to explore some specific ways of incorporating social interaction into the writing classroom in ways that support and promote the development of L2 students' written language.[1] The first goal is addressed directly in Chapter 2, which surveys the teaching and learning theories that lie behind the movement to transform the teaching of writing into a social event. To see how these theories play out in the classroom, Chapter 3 takes a close look at the cases of three individual ESL learners, each of whom uses talk differently in the process of acquiring written English.

To address the second goal, Chapters 4, 5, and 6 take a detailed look at the functions of talk in typical instructional environments involving L2 writers. They present specific strategies and techniques for putting dialogue to work in the service of L2 writing development—in the writing classroom (Chapter

---

[1]Only in the most rigidly controlled classroom can social interaction be avoided. The question is not one of getting students to talk but of creating an instructional atmosphere and specific tasks that successfully exploit the potential of talk to enhance the development of written language.

4), in the instructor's conference room or the writing center (Chapter 5), and in the written correspondence that passes between teacher and student (Chapter 6). The final chapter considers four critical questions that should be examined by any teacher who considers using the dialogic approach with his or her L2 writers.

The Argument for Dialogue

Douglas Barnes (1990), one of the most eloquent proponents of oral language as an educational tool, has claimed that *talk is a key factor* in all school learning. In a rhetorical question with direct relevance to our present concerns, he asks:

> How is it possible to introduce students to pre-existing systems and at the same time enable them to make independent choices?. . .the interaction between teacher and student through talk must play a central role in the strategies by which teachers seek to reconcile the two horns of the dilemma. (p. 44)

It will be our overall assumption that this dilemma and the response posed by Barnes apply to the teaching of writing (the "pre-existing system" in this case) and the development of individual learners' writing skills (the "independent choices") no less than to other content or skill areas in the school curriculum, and to L2 writers no less than to native speakers.

Whether the reader is a practicing foreign language or ESL teacher, a teacher of general composition, a teacher-in-training, or a teacher educator/researcher, it is hoped that the theoretical claims and practical suggestions made in the following chapters will provide fresh ways of looking at the uses of talk in the writing classroom, at our own social behavior as instructors, and at the nature of the tasks we set for our students as social learners.

In the spirit of James Britton, Douglas Barnes, Donald Rubin, and others, let's proceed on the grounds that by examining the nuts and bolts of social interaction between teachers and learners, we can identify some of the crucial elements involved in successful writing instruction for L2 learners.

Throughout, our general response to the problem of how teachers can best serve the needs of L2 learners in developing their writing skills is to approach the entire enterprise through dialogue.

Discussion Questions

1. An advanced L2 writer once told me, "If I don't talk, I don't learn." What could he have meant? What is your reaction to the claims made by the authors cited in this chapter that dialogue/social interaction lies at the heart of all learning? Is that too categorical a statement?

2. Do you think a writing pedagogy based on the dialogue approach would be suitable for mixed classes of L1 and L2 writers? Why or why not?

3. What dialogic strategies or techniques do you currently include in your own teaching? What made you decide to include these elements?

4. In your own experience, and as best as you can recollect, what role(s), if any, has social interaction played in your development as a writer?

5. What theories of writing/composition are you familiar with that support (or run counter to) the ideas put forward in this chapter?

Chapter 2
From Talking to Writing

"A dialogic perspective on development of literacy
portrays all language use, whether that of a child
or an adult, whether oral or written, as entering into
conversation with others."
(Ann Dyson, 1995, p. 39)

Sadiqa, a young woman from the Middle East, stands in front of her classmates in a basic-level ESL writing class. She displays a photograph of her father, a highway engineer, and briefly describes his life and work. The students listen attentively and take notes while she completes her extemporaneous speech, sometimes interrupting her with questions. After Sadiqa finishes, they break into small groups and talk over the thumbnail biography she has given, exchanging information and orally filling in the gaps in each other's notes. Later, the teacher asks the students to write individual paragraphs about Sadiqa's father, using their notes (and remembering to attach final –s to all third-person present tense verbs).

Of course, it's not only their written notes that the students rely on as they write their paragraphs about Sadiqa's father. They also use as a resource the questions, answers, and comments they have internalized, perhaps unconsciously, from their group discussions. They are using spoken as well as written language as input for their writing. When they get to the point of actually writing a paragraph, they have Sadiqa's voice in their ears to guide them, and they have the multiple voices of their classmates and their own as well—clarifying, correcting, asking, and retelling.

The students in Sadiqa's class used social interaction as a support for the development of their L2 writing skills. In a similar fashion, students in an advanced ESL academic writing class incorporate social interaction into their writing when they make use of suggestions offered by their peer revision groups to fine-tune second drafts of their essays. And something similar also occurs in a freshman composition class composed of both L1 and L2 writers, where students tell each other oral narratives, record and transcribe them, and then transform the oral versions into polished written essays (Loomis, 2003). In all these cases, L2 writers use their oral voices for the purpose of invention—to get their ideas flowing on paper (Rankin, 2001). By using spoken language to negotiate with others, they are bootstrapping themselves toward higher levels of proficiency in writing.

What accounts for the power of social talk to enhance the acquisition of writing by L2 learners? Indeed, what evidence is there that talk makes such a difference? The evidence comes from three main sources: *developmental theories of L1 and L2 writers, sociocultural theory and related research into the role of social interaction in teaching writing,* and *empirical studies of oral language use in L1 and L2 writing classrooms.* This chapter discusses each of these areas to develop an argument for the inclusion of social interaction in writing instruction for L2 learners. Finally, we use insights from all three areas to create a model for a dialogic writing classroom.

From Talking to Writing: Developmental Theories

Since the 1970s, researchers working in the area of childhood literacy have traced the important role that oral language plays in learning to write for native and non-native children (see an excellent review of this research in Dickinson, Wolf, & Stotsky, 1993). Children's early writing clearly reflects their spoken language in its reliance on sentence fragments linked with coordinating conjunctions like *and*; a high degree of personal involvement, indicated by frequent use of first- and second-person pronouns; a reliance on word repetition; and a focus on the here and now, signaled by extensive use of the present tense and the active voice (Elbow, 1985; Kantor & Rubin, 1981; Rubin, 1988).

Social conversation also serves as the source for many of the rhetorical strategies developed by young writers. The speaker's ability to provide information, to develop a topic, to shape a message to meet the expectations of a particular audience—all of these are aspects of conversation that transfer later into expository and persuasive writing. As Rubin, Goodman, and Hall (1990) note, "Most people learn about adapting to audiences, about collaborating, about exploring a topic and about communicator responsibility through spoken interaction" (p. 66).

Unlike speech, the development of literacy is not a universal phenomenon (Dickinson, Wolf, & Stotsky, 1993). Although virtually all normally developing children master an oral variety of their mother tongue, there is much more individual variation in the levels of competence that learners achieve in written language. Indeed, many children around the world never develop reading and writing skills at all. For those who do, the cognitive hurdle of moving from face-to-face dialogue to writing for an invisible audience of readers is one of the greatest they face (Bereiter & Scardamalia, 1982). Some writers never proceed beyond a "speech-written-down" style of writing; other writers, especially those who receive writing instruction as part of their schooling and who are exposed to large amounts of written text, begin to move away from their oral language through a process of *differentiation* (see Figure 1 and Kroll, 1981). With exposure to reading and writing, these writers start to pick up tricks of the literacy trade. Their writing gradually sheds its speech-like qualities as they become less dependent on a physically present audience. Their sentences increase in syntactic complexity, with greater use of subordinated and embedded clauses. The lexical density

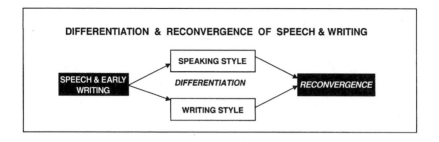

Figure 1. A differentiation model of speech and writing (adapted from Kroll, 1981).

of their writing increases as their vocabularies increase, and they try to avoid direct repetition of words through the use of synonyms and circumlocution. The active verbs of their speech give way to nominalizations and noun compounds (Halliday, 1989).

As their spoken and written styles diverge, the written texts they produce often seem stilted and awkward, as seen in this excerpt written by an undergraduate native speaker of English:

In the theory of interracial interactions we are taught the diversity between races is the beneficial difference....Stereotypes are a natural response in the situation of an unknown, but the willingness to allow the person to defend themselves [sic] against the accusations differentiates the usage of racial discrimination.

(from Szczepanski, 2003, p. 216)

Some writers may never develop beyond the differentiation stage. Others, especially those for whom writing plays an important role in their professional and personal lives, continue to refine their written styles throughout their adulthood, eventually achieving a *reconvergence* with their spoken style (Kroll, 1981). By selectively reintroducing speech-like elements into their writing, they enliven it and imbue it with a personal voice, as this composition teacher does in writing to his students:

> Your own voice is a great one—it's your essence. But, I'll level with you. There will be times when you will have to assume the formal voice of an academic paper whether you want to or not. And, in fact, there will be times when you'll choose to, because there is power involved in gaining the ability to choose how you appear to others. There are other times when you'll be able to play around more freely, especially in creative writing, where pushing the boundaries of voice is valued...your voice has a place in each of these forms of writing....

(from Szczepanski, 2003, pp. 215–216)

Fully developed L1 writers have a range of voices at their disposal, and as this instructor points out, they can assume a formal, impersonal style in their writing when the occasion calls for it.

If native speakers' writing styles vary widely by individuals, L2 writers represent an even more complicated picture. They typically bring a wider range of ages and life experiences to the classroom than do young native-speaker writers, and the development of their L2 writing and its relationship to their speech varies more widely. Some L2 writers follow the differentiation pattern of development as native speakers do, relying on their oral competence when they write. Examples of such L2 learners include those who emigrated to English-speaking countries as children or who, although born in an English-speaking country and educated in English-medium schools, are children of immigrants and speak a different first language at home—members of the so-called Generation 1.5 (Harklau, Losey, & Siegal, 1999). Like native speakers, these learners' proficiency in the spoken language is a crucial part of the foundation on which their writing develops.

But not all L2 writers rely on their oral competence to produce written texts in their second language. Some international students at U.S. universities, for example, may have English writing skills that are far more advanced than their spoken

English. Indeed, students whose previous contact with English has been mainly through reading and grammar instruction in their home countries may begin to develop their written English in the near absence of L2 oral skills (Harklau, 2002; Weissberg, 2000). Such students are not likely to rely on spoken English as a basis for their writing, at least not initially.

Whether or not an L2 student is orally fluent in the second language may not be the critical issue for teachers of L2 writers, however. As Rubin, Goodrum, and Hall (1990) note, all ESL students are orally fluent in at least one other language, and they may use invention and rhetorical strategies in their written English that come from that knowledge. Skillful teachers can help their L2 writers learn to trust their oral knowledge, whether L1- or L2-based, in developing their writing (Blanton, 1992; Mangelsdorf, 1989). The talk-write activity described at the beginning of this chapter is one example of a teacher's attempt to do just that. We will discuss others later in this chapter.

Styles of Talking and Writing

In addition to a range of spoken and written language styles, many native speakers also develop a keen sense of stylistic appropriateness; that is, they have a sense of which style is best for a given speaking or writing situation. However, it is not the case, as linguists like Michael Halliday (1987) and Wallace Chafe (1982) have pointed out, that native speakers' speech is always casual and their writing is always formal. Some spoken language can be highly formal, almost written-like (e.g., a televised discussion among foreign policy experts); at the same time, some written language can be extremely casual, such as an e-mail message sent to a close friend. In place of a simplistic speaking-writing dichotomy, Halliday and Chafe proposed a functional-structural continuum of language styles, running between two poles—one more careful and monitored, the other more spontaneous and casual (see Figure 2). Between the two poles exists a range of hybrid forms, containing a mixture of spontaneous and carefully monitored language styles—an extemporaneous classroom lecture being one

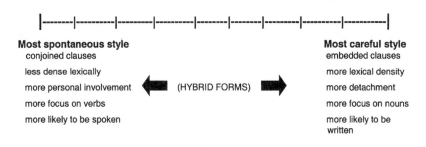

Figure 2. A functional-structural continuum of language styles (based on Halliday, 1987, and Chafe, 1982).

example (Barton, 2004). *Hybrid forms* are discussed again in Chapter 6.

Depending on their linguistic sophistication, native speakers may use a wider or narrower range of the styles available along this continuum. L2 writers and speakers will likely have a more restricted range at their disposal, although even novice L2 writers may have a sense of the textual differences between careful and casual styles (such as the avoidance of contractions in formal written English). And L2 writers who are highly literate in their own language may have a well-developed sensitivity to stylistic appropriateness, even if they don't yet have the linguistic means to display it when they write in their second language.

From Talking to Writing: The Sociocultural Explanation

In addition to developmental studies of L1 and L2 writers, the connections between talk and writing have also been explored in the works of scholars associated with the Russian psychologist Lev Vygotsky, referred to collectively as sociocultural theorists (Lantolf, 2000; Wertsch, 1991). For socioculturalists, speech is "the tool of tools" (Luria, as cited in Lee & Smagorinsky, 2000, p. 2); it is the key to the child's development of cognitive skills in general and literacy skills in particular.

Working in the first two decades after the Russian revolution, Vygotsky conducted experiments in which he observed children's behavior when they were presented with a variety of cognitively demanding tasks. On the basis of these studies, he concluded that children internalize their social talk as *inner speech,* a silent, abbreviated form of oral language that they use as a cognitive tool for solving problems. In fact, Vygotsky claimed that all higher cognitive functions, including writing, develop out of social interaction internalized as "inner speech" (Vygotsky, 1986).

A. R. Luria (1969) and A. A. Leont'yev (1969), two other Soviet psychologists associated with Vygotsky, made the speech-writing connection explicit. They claimed that inner speech is the initial basis for writing and that novice writers use it to produce a kind of "written speech." According to this view, emergent writing is actually *externalized inner speech.* Expert writers become so practiced at utilizing inner speech that the texts they produce feed back into their planning processes, creating an internal dialogue that assists them in writing more text (see Figure 3). Kenneth Bruffee (1995) captures this idea succinctly when he writes, "If thought is internalized public and social talk, then writing is internalized talk made public and social again. If thought is internalized conversation, then writing is internalized conversation reexternalized" (pp. 90–91).

Literacy researchers have used Vygotsky's theoretical framework to study the development of writing in both L1

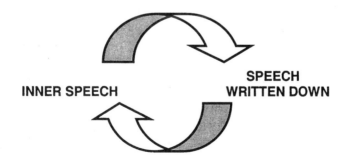

Figure 3. The internal dialogue between speech and writing (after Luria, 1969, and Leont'yev, 1969).

and L2 users (Lee & Smagorinsky, 2000). For example, several researchers working with L2 writers have used as their methodology a technique called *think-aloud protocols,* in which they ask their subjects to talk about their writing and their writing processes while they are actually engaged in a writing task. The subjects' protocols are tape-recorded for later analysis. Some researchers have suggested that *think-alouds* are in fact the outward manifestation of L2 writers' inner speech, a kind of oral window into a writer's composing process (Pavlenko & Lantolf, 2000; Prior, 2001; Woodall, 2002).

Exactly how L2 writers might make use of inner speech in the act of writing is an intriguing question. There is experimental evidence from a study of students writing in Spanish as a second language that suggests that L2 writers make greater use of inner speech as the difficulty of their writing tasks increase (Roebuck, 2000). Another study with ESL writers found that more proficient writers relied on inner speech less than did lower proficiency students (McCafferty, 1994). It is still not clear, however, exactly how L2 writers of different proficiencies make use of inner speech as a resource when they write.

Vygotsky's ideas have played a major role in prompting writing teachers and composition theorists to focus on collaborative learning as one way to promote the speaking-thinking-writing connection for student writers (Lee & Smagorinsky, 2000). When students collaborate in pairs on a writing project, some asymmetry in their relative levels of skill mastery normally becomes evident. That is, one member of the pair is usually a bit more advanced in a particular literacy skill than is the partner. When this is the case, verbal interaction may give rise to a natural tutorial phenomenon that Vygotsky called the "zone of proximal development" (ZPD), defined as "the difference between what the learner can accomplish unaided and what he or she can do with assistance" (as quoted in Lantolf, 2000, p. 17). For example, Amy Ohta (2000, 2001) studied pairs of U.S. college students engaged in a Japanese-as-an-L2 translation task. She found that one student in a pair sometimes took it upon himself or herself to act as a tutor and assist the less proficient writer to accomplish part of the task by building a *conversational scaffold*. Similar scaffolding behavior has been observed with pairs of students learning French as a second language (Swain & Lapkin, 1998) and with pairs of ESL writers engaged in a revision task (De Guerrero & Villamil, 2000). A more detailed look at collaborative talk, scaffolding, and the ZPD is presented in Chapter 5.

Because it crystallizes the notion that writing is a social phenomenon, Vygotsky's sociocultural perspective is central to the practical issues of teaching L2 writing and to our argument for creating a dialogic atmosphere in the writing classroom. His ideas have become increasingly popular in composition circles, and teachers of both L1 and L2 writers are making practical use of the concepts of the ZPD, inner speech, and the notion that the learner's social communication precedes and paves the way for the development of literacy (Moll, 1989). The next section explores some of the ways in which writing teachers have put these ideas into practice.

Talking and Writing at School: Some Classroom Examples

Even before Vygotsky's theories became popular, literacy researchers were already aware of the strong connection between talking and writing for beginning writers. In early research on the development of writing in school, Britton, Burgess, Martin, McLeod, and Rosen (1975) showed how children writing in the elementary grades rely on speech-based modes of rhetoric—personal narrative and expressive writing, such as letters and journal entries. More recently, the link among social talk, learning, and writing has been exploited in L1 and L2 classrooms in a variety of ways. Teachers and researchers like Anne Dyson (1988) working in the elementary grades have found that early school writing has a strong social function for children—that, like conversation, writing is often a function of the child's social life at school. It can be a direct reflection of, and at times an agent in, the personal relationships children have with their classmates, playmates, and teachers. Indeed, writing has a way of evolving out of children's oral communication whether it is called for in the school curriculum or not. In bilingual programs, where children in the early grades may not yet be required to write in their second language, written English has been observed to develop spontaneously as an offshoot of children's social network inside and outside the classroom (Hudelson, 2005).

Some teachers in the lower grades deliberately involve their students in social activities to support their literacy development. Anne Dyson (2000) describes an "author's theater" project in an urban elementary school classroom in which students write dramatic dialogues to be acted out by classmates playing themselves. Rubin and Kantor (1984) describe a fifth-grade class in which writing and group social activities are linked throughout the entire day's lessons in all subject areas—math, science, geography, social studies, and literature. Gordon Wells (2000) describes elementary and middle school classrooms in which groups of students work collaboratively on projects in literature, math, and science, and then use writing as a cumulative group activity to help each other make sense of the lesson content.

Teachers have used similar techniques with non–native speaking children in the early grades. One fourth grade teacher of bilingual students established a collaborative, student-centered writing class in which the children were free to set their own agendas when commenting on each other's writing (Gutierrez, 1994). In an earlier study, Wells (1990) describes another teacher who organized her non-native speaking students in groups by common interests and helped them develop a three week–long project involving reading, writing, drawing, mapmaking, and model building.

The project described by Wells provides an excellent model for the use of classroom talk as a scaffold to help emergent L2 writers move into school writing. The children started by writing preliminary questions they wanted to answer during the course of the project. The teacher then met with each group, reviewing the questions and helping each to plan its project. When the projects were completed, the teacher asked the children to write about their experience—how they started on the project, what difficulties they overcame, and how satisfied they were with the outcome. Finally, in order to help the children become more aware of their own writing and thinking processes, the teacher met with each group again to help them talk reflectively about their experiences with the project.

These teachers did not view their students' oral language as a source of interference in their writing, but rather as a resource to be tapped. Their approaches were dialogic in that they deliberately sought to retain the influence of conversational give-and-take at critical points in their writing lessons. It is this dialogic model of teaching writing that we will be exploring in detail in subsequent chapters. For now, let us consider (1) how far the dialogue model can be extended in terms of age and sophistication of students and (2) how it might best be applied in writing classes with L2 writers.

The dialogic model has been put into practice in classrooms beyond the early grades. At the college level, some composition teachers have adopted a dialogue approach in an attempt to facilitate their students' composing processes. James Zebroski (1994) describes how in one college writing classroom, speaking and writing alternated in "leading" each other. Sometimes his students' oral invention ran ahead of their writing, in which case social talk pushed their writing along. At other times in the same class, and sometimes among the same student groups, writing led speech—that is, the students were able to produce written texts faster and more easily than they could produce related ideas orally. Classrooms that follow the dialogic model allow for this synergy of conversation and writing to take place.

Stock and Robinson (1990) describe another college writing course designed to bring dialogue into students' writing processes. They injected opportunities for conversation at critical points throughout the course by moving the instructor away from center stage to a more facilitative role and turning much of the class work over to student writing groups. In addition to revising and editing drafts, the groups also explored potential topics with each other before they did any writing. Then students prepared "dialog papers" for their groups to get feedback on ideas for upcoming writing assignments (p. 167). Stock and Robinson claim that with the writing groups as their primary audience, students developed a heightened sense of their readers' expectations. They learned "how to tell a story...what to put in, what to leave out, what to expand and what to compress, what to connect and how" (p. 222). The exploratory talk that students used in their writing groups carried over to student-teacher writing conferences and later to whole-class discussions about the completed essays.

College ESL writing instructors put this same dialogic approach to work when they organize class activities around collaborative writing groups that produce multiple-author or group texts. For example, Blanton (1992) and Hirvela (1999) describe oral-based activities in which groups of students jointly compose a reflective essay in response to a text that they have all read. In this task, students function as each other's peer reviewers and as coauthors. Hirvela (1999) points out that the principal benefit of collaborative group writing is that students are able to talk about the process as they engage in it. They make explicit for each other and for themselves what they already know and where the gaps in their knowledge lie. Oral tasks like this can raise students' level of awareness of their own strategies for solving writing problems, strategies that may be unconscious and underutilized by writers who work alone.

These glimpses of dialogic writing classrooms demonstrate that the talking-writing connection is not just a theoretical construct. In real writing classrooms at all levels, dialogue and social interaction can play a crucial role in supporting L1 and L2 learners as they develop their writing skills. However, the dialogic writing class doesn't just happen; teachers must make a systematic effort to put this kind of instruction into practice. The last part of this chapter presents a general plan for developing a dialogic style of instruction, one that permeates nearly every aspect of the writing class.

Creating Dialogic Writing Lessons: A General Scheme

In every writing lesson there are critical moments when social interaction can help students overcome writing barriers and reach new levels of proficiency. The dialogic teacher recognizes these moments, plans for them, and exploits them (Wells, 1990, p. 396). Some dialogic moments are fortuitous—for example, when a student comes to the teacher with a half-finished piece of writing and asks, "What should I write next?" or "Does this sentence sound right here?" Other moments are embedded in normal lesson routines. In order to build a strong dialogue component into writing instruction, teachers must plan ahead for these moments and also must be ready to take advantage of the serendipitous ones. As Kenneth Bruffee (1995) notes,

> Our task must involve engaging students in conversation at as many points in the writing process as possible...we should contrive to ensure that the conversation is similar in as many ways as possible to the way we would like them eventually to write. (p. 91)

To create dialogic instruction for L2 writers, we begin by identifying some of the primary opportunities for dialogue in typical writing lessons. At least five come to mind: *pre-writing talk* (whole-class discussion and/or in groups), *invention talk, prompting during writing, responding to students' writing,* and *reflecting on completed writing tasks.* Figure 4 illustrates these opportunities for dialogue at critical moments during instruction on a typical, multi-step writing assignment.

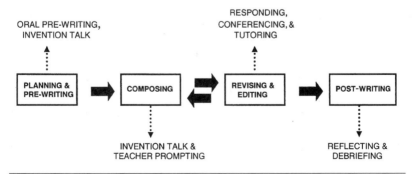

Figure 4. Opportunities for dialogue in the writing classroom.

Pre-Writing Talk

In the dialogic model, preliminary talk functions as a scaffold for L2 students as they struggle to come to terms with the requirements of a new writing assignment. When teachers discuss writing assignments with students before the actual work of writing begins, they help them to frame the task in terms of their previous knowledge and experience. This is the dialogic writing teacher's equivalent of a basic instructional strategy common to all areas of the school curriculum: The teacher starts with what students already know, helps them to realize that they know it, and then shows them how it connects to new information or tasks (Harklau, 1999). Depending on the students' age and L2 proficiency, this might be accomplished by explaining the general specifications of the assignment; describing a picture; or discussing a reading selection or a video, a recent story in the news, a current movie, an incident at school, or an instructional point from a previous class or from the textbook—any topic that creates links to students' previous knowledge and that provides background information needed for the assignment.

Invention Talk

Invention talk also occurs before students begin drafting their assignment, but it serves a different function from pre-writing talk. Rather than framing the assignment in broad terms or suggesting possible topics, invention talk generates specific linguistic material—words, phrases, and even whole sentences—for possible incorporation into students' writing. Invention talk can be done as a whole-class discussion or carried out in small groups or pairs. Formally organized invention tasks may involve students discussing a set of questions intended to help generate ideas for the coming writing task or sharing the results of written brainstorms they have already completed. Oral invention occurs when students presenting the idea content for a subsequent writing task (as Sadiqa did in the activity described at the beginning of this chapter), or when a student and teacher meet in conference to explore and develop a topic. Invention talk can also occur while students are actually engaged in the process of producing text, as in the case of cooperative writing activities or impromptu student-teacher interactions during in-class writing assignments.

From a Vygotskian perspective, the dialogue resulting from pre-writing and invention talk is an important resource for helping writers to generate inner speech. From a Bakhtinian point of view (see Wertsch, 1991, and Hall, Vitanova, & Marchenkova, 2005, for excellent discussions of Bakhtin's theories), invention talk contributes to the multiplicity of voices that is necessary for the genesis of all written language. Regardless of one's theoretical orientation, time devoted to pre-writing and invention talk is time well spent for L2 students; it helps them internalize the general guidelines, idea content, and linguistic material that they will need to accomplish the writing task ahead.

Prompting

First referred to in the L1 writing literature as "procedural facilitation" (Bereiter & Scardamalia, 1982), oral prompting helps student writers to get past the rough spots when they are actually in the act of composing. Prompts are verbal nudges given to the writer by a tutor, a teacher, or by a fellow student. They are similar to the utterances used in casual conversations when one speaker urges another forward to keep the talk going. And, as in casual conversation, prompts in the writing class are often phrased as questions *(Can you tell me a little more about that? Could you explain what you mean by that? Can you give an example of that?)* that teachers or tutors might ask when a writer comes forward with a problem sentence or a case of writer's block. Framing the prompt as a question helps to keep the support dialogic.

Prompts are sometimes solicited by the student, as in cases where a student approaches the teacher for help during an in-class writing assignment. Student-solicited prompts are particularly effective from a classroom discourse perspective since they provide the student rather than the teacher with the opportunity to initiate the dialogue and set the topic. (This and other aspects of classroom discourse will be explored more fully in Chapter 4.) Regardless of the source of the prompts, the long-term benefit is that with repeated exposure to oral nudges from teachers, tutors, and peers, student writers may eventually internalize and access them as facilitaing procedures when they are writing on their own (Bereiter & Scardamalia, 1982).

Responding to Students' Writing

Responding to students' writing is one of the richest opportunities for involving L2 writers in dialogue both in and outside the classroom. With the advent of the process approach to teaching writing, oral response to students' texts has become one of the most common dialogic activities in the writing classroom (Liu & Hansen, 2002). Peer response groups or student writers working in pairs may provide oral feedback to individual students about their drafts, or they may comment on texts that have been written collaboratively (Hirvela, 1999). Oral response also takes place in writing tutorials and teacher-student conferences. However, responses to students' writing need not always be oral; in fact, the most common responses are the comments that teachers write on students' drafts. Later chapters will examine both types of response to L2 student writing, written and oral, and their potential for enhancing the dialogic atmosphere of the writing classroom.

Reflective Talk

In the dialogic writing class, the talk continues even when the writing assignment is finished (Wells, 1990). Reflective talk about completed writing assignments can take place during teacher-led, whole-class discussions in which the teacher debriefs the class with a discussion of the problems encountered while working on the assignment and the solutions that were discovered. Reflective talk can also occur in workshop groups where students analyze and critique sample papers written by their classmates and in individual teacher-student consultations. Oral reflection activities help writers to bring closure to a writing assignment by stepping back from it, evaluating its outcomes, and assessing their own progress. Teachers can also use reflective talk activities to create transitions between one writing assignment and the next. Both functions are especially helpful for L2 writers.

Conclusion

The five dialogic functions discussed here by no means exhaust the possibilities for purposeful talk in the writing class, but they hint at the possibilities, and most important they provide a framework that writing teachers can identify additional opportunities for dialogue. Before concluding this preliminary discussion, two caveats deserve mention.

As noted earlier, *dialogic writing classrooms don't happen by accident.* They require not only careful planning but also a willingness on the part of the teacher to relinquish a measure of control over classroom discourse. Each of the classrooms described in this chapter were managed by teachers who were not afraid to give students a greater say in deciding who talks when and how much, in determining what is talked about, and even at times in deciding what the agenda for a writing activity will be.

Second, *although classroom talk about writing is usually teacher guided, it is nonetheless unpredictable.* Teachers will generally have an instructional goal in mind for an oral activity, but they must recognize that there are as many ways to reach the goal as there are students participating in the conversation. They must also be prepared for the fact that some students may try to reorient, subvert, or reject outright the teacher's goals in order to accomplish their own. Consequently, the dialogic writing teacher must be prepared to evaluate at any given moment the value and consequences of a given oral activity. More will be said about this topic in the final chapter.

Teachers are not the only ones who may need to reevaluate their own behaviors in the dialogic writing class. Second language students are often silent collaborators in maintaining traditional, teacher-directed, transmission-style instruction in their classrooms (Thonus, 1999a). Student writers from cultures where authoritarian classrooms predominate may feel especially uncomfortable and even threatened by oral activities in which they are encouraged to express themselves, even to the point of disagreeing with classmates or with the teacher. And many students, regardless of their cultural background, may at first see no positive relationship between time spent engaging in oral activities and learning to write. They may see the teacher's invitations to participate in conversational tasks as a sign that the class is not a serious one or that the teacher does not have a firm grasp of the subject matter. To address these issues effectively, the dialogic writing teacher must be prepared to play multiple roles, acting at various times as a guide, a coach, a moderator, and a coparticipant in the classroom dialogue.

This chapter has established a rationale for the deliberate and principled use of oral dialogue in classes with L2 writers. A general scheme for bringing this about has been sketched. Now the dialogic writing classroom can be defined as a place where oral language is recognized as a developmental springboard into writing for L2 as well as L1 writers, and where a multitude of opportunities exist—some planned, some fortuitous—for dialogue to serve the purposes of writing instruction. Subsequent chapters will look in more detail at ways in which L2 students, with their teachers' assistance, can take full advantage of the opportunities provided by dialogue to develop their writing skills. Next, however, we examine critical individual differences among L2 writers that may affect their experiences and success in a dialogic learning environment.

Suggested Tasks

1. Observe a writing class in which L2 or foreign language students are enrolled. Notice the roles that oral language plays in the class environment and in the tasks that students are asked to do. Try to match the functions of classroom talk to the categories discussed in this chapter and shown in Figure 3.

2. Read carefully a few papers written by L2 students in a class you are teaching or observing. Try to determine to what extent these students are writing with their English "speaking voice" or to what degree they have developed a distinct written register.

3. Reflect on your own cognitive process when you write. Do you hear your own inner speech as you compose? Are there some writing tasks in which your inner speech does *not* seem to be active?

Chapter 3

ESL Writers and Speakers:
A World of Individual Differences

*"Why shouldn't students' acquisition of an L2 take
place through literate as well as oral modalities?"*
(Linda Harklau, 2002, p. 337)

When Sadiqa has finished telling the class about her father the highway engineer (see Chapter 2), the teacher asks her classmates to break into small groups and compare the notes they have taken during her talk. They are asked to check the accuracy of their information, and where there are disagreements they must try to reach a consensus on precisely what Sadiqa told them during her presentation. Students who didn't catch all of Sadiqa's information now work to complete their notes with the help of other classmates. During their discussions, the teacher sits to one side while Sadiqa moves from group to group, repeating or clarifying factual information when the students are unable to reach agreement on their notes.

The ESL students in this class approach the speaking part of this "talk-write" task in different ways. Some converse actively with other members of their group; some listen attentively, occasionally making adjustments in their notes as the group carries on its discussion; still others appear not to be participating much in the group work but are already starting to write the paragraph that they assume will be the follow-up assignment.

Indeed, the teacher finally does ask the students to write their own brief paragraphs about Sadiqa's father based on what they remember from her presentation, the information in their notes, and their group discussions. When the teacher reviews the resulting paragraphs after class, he notices some interesting differences. Aside from the expected discrepancies from one student's paper to another in grammatical control, vocabulary range, and orthography, their paragraphs also differ in the way they "sound." The teacher notices that one student's paper reads as though the student herself were speaking directly to him; he can almost hear her voice coming through the sentences. It strikes him that she writes English very much as she speaks it, with the same characteristic errors and habitual expressions.

Another paper catches his attention because this student's written language is so different from his speech. The writing is in general more accurate and fleshed out than the student's often telegraphic spoken English. Syntactic elements usually missing from his speech—articles, prepositions, pronouns, verb endings—are mostly present in his written sentences. There is even the hint of a formal written register created by the use of the passive voice and the order of clauses in complex sentences. The rest of the student papers fall somewhere between these two extremes of speech-like and writing-like texts.

All the students in this class are high-beginners in English, and all of them have similar scores on a standardized test of English proficiency. All have limited fluency and accuracy in oral English. All have been exposed to the same language instruction since the course began. All heard the same student presentation, and all had the opportunity to share their notes on it with others in the class. What accounts for the wide variation in the way their written language "sounds"?

Many factors beyond the immediate instructional setting influence the writing development of second language learners, and some of them involve the influence of the learner's oral language (see Figure 5). For some L2 writers, those whom Joy Reid (1998) has labeled "ear learners," the oral influences

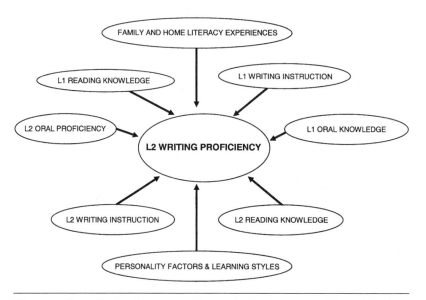

Figure 5. Contributing factors to a learner's development of L2 writing.

are especially strong; for others, "eye learners," the oral influences are eclipsed by their previous experiences with literacy activities in general and with L1 writing in particular. This chapter looks at how different students develop expertise in L2 writing in relation to their L2 speech. We will see that some rely heavily on their oral knowledge of the second language, while others seem to develop their writing skills independent of their speech—almost as if they were learning to write in an oral vacuum. Finally, we will return to the developmental models of literacy we discussed in the previous chapter and reevaluate them from the perspective of individual L2 learner differences. First, however, we examine three of Sadiqa's classmates—all high-beginner ESL writers sharing the same first language, but taking three quite different paths toward proficiency in written English.

Case 1: Francisco—A Speaker Learns to Write

Francisco is a 19-year-old high school graduate from Mexico. He is a sociable, outgoing young man who gets along easily with his classmates and with native English speakers. He finds it easy to make small talk in English with friends around campus, chatting about sports, girlfriends, the weather, etc. He even reports having dreams about conversing in English. His spoken English displays many syntactic and phonological inaccuracies, but he is generally communicative, and his fluency and accuracy are steadily improving.

Francisco is a graduate of a prestigious private preparatory school in a large city in northern Mexico where his father is a businessman. He has a medical condition that necessitates frequent visits to a city on the U.S.-Mexican border for treatment. While there, he usually stays with monolingual English-speaking relatives. His usual reading in Spanish is restricted to the daily newspaper. During his student years in Mexico he read in English only infrequently, and he had no previous experience writing English beyond the sentence level. However, he took courses in Spanish composition *(redacción)* during his preparatory years. He plans to get a bachelor's degree in accounting but at present is taking only intensive English courses.

When the instructor looks at Francisco's paper, he finds no great lexical or syntactic differences between his writing and his speech. Francisco's written English is characterized by the same chatty, conversational features that the teacher hears in his spoken English. These are clearly evident in a sample of Francisco's writing taken later in the same course.

The teacher's writing prompt: *Every city or town has social or economic problems. Identify one such problem in your home community and discuss ways in which it might be solved.*

Well I came from Chihuahua, Chih. Mexico, I'm Francisco and I talk to you about the problems that we have in Mexico.

In Mexico all the states have the same problem, this problem is the govern.

This is the first problem in Mexico, the second is the work and we have others problems but this two are very importants.

With this new president we can do it, because with the others

presidents of the country we can't do it....

I'm very angry because Mexico have all,

For example: Beaches, a beautiful citys like Guadalajara, Monterrey,

Guanajuato, etc. We produce a lot products for example: Petroleo,

Beef, Chile, Cacao, etc. Well we have all and we can't be able to be

the second or third country of the world.

Well that's all, I don't know what is the future of Mexico but I

hope that we can resolve our problems.

See you later.

It sounds to the instructor like Francisco is "talking his way" through this early attempt at written English. But, as Figure 5 suggests, there are probably other influences at work on his L2 writing. Francisco has told his instructor that he has no trouble producing paragraphs, topic sentences, and thesis statements in his writing because he studied all these things in Spanish, but he has also said that he gets nervous and forgets what he knows about composition when he writes in English. The instructor does note some influences of formal composition in Francisco's writing—a three-part, proto-essay structure and punctuated lists (of products) and enumeration (of the problems faced by his country). But on the whole, Francisco's written English appears to be based on his oral knowledge of the language.

Francisco tells his teacher that he normally "thinks in English" while writing. He doesn't like to translate from Spanish because the resulting prose "sounds bad," although he was taught to use this method in his English classes in Mexico. He reports that the only time he resorts to Spanish while writing for this class is when he can't think of a word or an appropriate grammatical structure in English.

During the course, the instructor notices that Francisco's written English begins to develop the sound of a written register. The contractions and speech idioms slowly drop away and are replaced by a less personal style of sentences organized into paragraphs. Francisco begins to brainstorm and outline before writing his drafts, and after drafting he checks his papers for accuracy of spelling and grammar. By the end of the course, his writing will have lost many of its speech-like characteristics, and he will have begun to adopt the impersonal language and conventionalized rhetorical features of academic essay writing that the instructor is presenting in class.

Francisco's case is interesting because, at least in the initial stages of learning English, he has greater comfort and fluency in oral English than in writing. Having neither highly developed composition skills nor a sense of written register, Francisco uses his oral language to support and inform his writing. He is a rapid L2 acquirer, however, and as he progresses through the semester both his oral and written English show evidence of continuous innovation and improvement. His instructor is interested to note that the new syntactic and lexical items that Francisco adopts usually appear in his speech several weeks before they occur in his writing.

Case 2: Oscar—A Writer Tries to Speak

Francisco's classmate Oscar presents an entirely different profile of an L2 writer. Oscar is 32 years old, married, and has a daughter in pre-school. Before entering the intensive English course, he was a professor and researcher in electrical engineering at a Mexican university, and he has come to the United States to pursue a doctorate in the same field. Although Oscar doesn't come from a family of avid readers or writers, he enjoys writing very much. He says it's a way for him to "show his mind." He received no instruction in composition in Mexico after secondary school, but as part of his university work he had to do a significant amount of academic writing in Spanish: technical articles, research proposals, and research reports. He has several scholarly publications to his credit. Oscar also assisted his own undergraduate students with their own report writing. As an undergraduate himself, he wrote for his school newspaper, and he had considered a career in journalism at one point. More recently, in addition to his scholarly publications in engineering, he has tried his hand at humanistic writing in Spanish, producing essays on religion, literature, and politics.

Oscar is also an enthusiastic reader. Before he started his doctorate, he was reading as many as 50 books a year. In his *preparatorio* (high school) years he read fiction, science fiction, Mexican history and culture, and Roman history. He says that now, being away from home, it is even more important for him to keep up on events and social issues in his country.

Oscar had no more than the usual exposure to formal English study in his years as a student in Mexico—about one course a year, with an emphasis on grammar. He read a substantial amount of technical material in English before coming to the United States, as well as articles from *Time* and *Newsweek*, books on social topics, and occasionally poetry. But he had no training or experience in English writing other than grammar exercises.

In class, Oscar's demeanor is also very different from Francisco's. He sits in the rear of the classroom and is extremely quiet. He is not an enthusiastic participant in small group or pair activities, and he often looks bored. He has trouble understanding the teacher's oral instructions for written homework assignments and consequently sometimes fails to hand them in. When he speaks, his English is broken and hesitant, and he displays none of Francisco's social garrulousness. His voice quality is strained, and it appears that speaking is almost painful for him. He tells the instructor that he speaks English very little outside of class and almost never with native speakers. He reports that pronunciation and listening are his weakest areas, along with a limited vocabulary. "I have my verbs!" he says ironically, referring to his small stock of content words.

With this in mind, the instructor reads through Oscar's paragraph response to the "one problem in your community" prompt with some surprise. His writing is fluent and grammatically accurate. Spelling and punctuation are nearly flawless, and his placement in a high-beginner ESL class belies his large English vocabulary:

One of the principal problems in Mexico is Education. The government has said many things about the reason because publical education has a low academical level in the country. Since twenty years ago each minister of Education has becoming his personal fight against the problem, but without any solution still. Maybe the principal cause of the situation is the economical status of the professors. A professor in graduate level has a payment of 8000 dollars for a year. In the lowest levels, the salary is worst. The planning staff of the education Ministry has this problem in his mind, but other problem obstructs the solution....

The instructor hears little of Oscar's speaking voice in the sentences of this paper. In fact, it sounds almost as if it had been written by another student. Despite the errors and lack of idiom, Oscar's paper, like nearly all his written work throughout the course, exhibits a strong sense of academic writing—from the establishment of the topic in the first sentence and its subsequent logical development to the depersonalized voice of the author.

Oscar is acutely aware of his own abilities and problems in English. In addition to the self-analysis of his oral English previously mentioned, he says that writing is much easier for him than speaking. He has a well-developed strategy for planning and developing a writing topic, which is to choose a principal point, or "objective," and then construct "variations" around it. He reports that he does his preliminary planning in Spanish and then switches to English to find specific words, phrases, and expressions as he transcribes.

Throughout the ESL course, Oscar's written English continues to grow in fluency, accuracy, and expressiveness. Some of his journal entries are so well—even poetically—written that as the instructor reads them, he feels sometimes that he is a party to Oscar's innermost thoughts. His oral language, on the other hand, develops at a very different rate. By the end of the course he will still be confusing pronoun number, gender, and case, often reducing all personal pronouns to *he,* even plurals. He will continue to have difficulty using simple verb tenses, and his overall grammatical accuracy will still be far below that of his writing.

At the end of the course Oscar reflects in his journal on his frustrations at trying to converse in English:

It's traumatic for people when they come to U.S. and think that they know the English language and when speak with another people don't understand anything....Why can't I understand anything in the streets? The answer is easy: Most of people don't speak the language which they studied in books, because the English like any other language is changing every day.

Oscar will eventually develop into a competent academic writer of English, writing a doctoral dissertation in electrical and computer engineering. During the ESL course, however, his instructor will notice that, while Oscar continues to add new grammatical structures and sophisticated vocabulary to his written repertoire, his conversational English never develops much beyond the dysfluent, telegraphic style of speech he displayed at the beginning of the course.

Case 3: Manuela—A Case of Symmetrical Development

In our first case, Francisco appeared to be using his knowledge of and proficiency in spoken English to "push" his acquisition of L2 writing. The second case offered a contrasting phenomenon: Oscar developed a high level of fluency and accuracy in written English without much effect on his speaking at all. Both Francisco and Oscar represent **asymmetrical development.** The former uses one production modality to push the other one along; the latter develops one modality almost in the absence of the other. When we look at our third ESL learner, Manuela, we see a different developmental pattern.

Manuela entered the intensive English course as an exchange student from northern Spain. She is older than the typical undergraduate transfer student, having worked in private business for several years before returning to school. She is taking the intensive English course in addition to two university courses—one in business management and the other in industrial engineering. She plans to return to Spain at the end of the semester to finish her degree, which focuses on online marketing and sales. As an upper-division student at a European university, Manuela has done a lot of academic writing in Spanish but has had very little, if any, experience with written English before taking the ESL course.

Although her stay in the United States will be brief, Manuela has thrown herself into the social life of the university. She is involved in international student organizations, plays soccer on an intramural team, and "parties" regularly. She has a wide circle of friends including other international students and many native English speakers. Her social skills are readily apparent in the classroom, where she not only participates actively in group work but often takes over as leader.

The instructor has noted that Manuela is an extremely adept language learner. She picks up idiomatic, conversational English rapidly, and she gets some of the highest scores in the class on her written assignments. Her writing is clear, concise, and marked by few mechanical errors. Her repertoire of English grammatical structures is expanding rapidly, and the improvement is apparent in both her writing and her speech.

Responding to the teacher's prompt, *Would it help you to write better in this course if the class was held in a computer laboratory?* Manuela writes the following response:

I think that for a class like this, the computer is not necessary at all. Even I think that the computer is not good because it makes the student so lazy because of grammatical and spelling tools. This kind of tools sometimes cause that the student do not pay attention to grammatical details because the computer can do that for him. As a consequence, the student do not assimilate some concepts (for example, I am not sure that the word "necessary" is accurately written, but it does not mind because the computer will warn me about). Besides, the computers are not reliable. I missed two assignments in this class because of them!

The instructor can hear more of the student's speaking voice in this paragraph than he could in Oscar's but not as clearly as in Francisco's writing. This sample strikes him as showing evidence of both written and oral influences. The beginning and end of the paragraph are personalized, while the middle section is objective and analytical. Manuela has included several transition expressions common in written English, and she is careful to include an example to support her assertion that computers prevent students from learning. At the same time, the misused expression *it does not mind* probably comes from speech *(I don't mind),* and the paragraph ends with an ironic joke, as would an oral narrative.

As Manuela continues to acquire English, her writing becomes more academic sounding, yet there are still traces of humor and the surprising, sometimes disconnected, juxtaposition of ideas found in her speech. Manuela tells her instructor that when composing in English she relies heavily on her knowledge of composition techniques in Spanish, but she uses translation as a tool only when looking for an appropriate word. Otherwise she does not rely much on her dictionary or her Spanish lexicon. She reports that she "hears in her mind" many of the English sentences she writes just before putting them down on paper. The instructor notes that many of the syntactic and lexical innovations in Manuela's English appear in both her spoken and written production at about the same time. In contrast to Francisco and Oscar, Manuela's L2 speech and writing appear to be developing in parallel, with neither modality consistently pushing or leading the other.

A Model or Models?

Many writing instructors have had experience with students like Francisco, Oscar, and Manuela. They are neither extreme nor exaggerated cases. They are not difficult students to teach; they are willing, motivated, and bright, but they follow distinctly different paths in their acquisition of written English as a second language. And they highlight the important role that individual differences play in the acquisition of an L2 and in the development of L2 writing in particular.

Most writing teachers are aware of differences among their students in terms of proficiency, learning styles, and developmental rates. What they may not be so conscious of are the modality (speaking versus writing) discrepancies that exist for individual L2 learners. The issues addressed in the remainder of this chapter are (1) how to reconcile individual differences, like those we have seen in our three ESL learners, with the theoretical models of oral and written language development introduced in Chapter 2, and (2) how to reconfigure the writing class as a potential **modality equalizer** for L2 writers—a place where oral language and written language tasks are balanced and sequenced so that students' strengths in one modality can support their development in the other.

The three ESL writers described here should prompt us to take another look at our assumptions about how learners develop writing proficiency in a second language. We recall that both the developmental models of writing discussed in the previous chapter take speech as their point of departure. Kroll's (1981) model proposes that a child's development of writing transforms over time (and as a consequence of schooling) from a speech-like stage into a differentiated phase in which the learner produces quite distinct spoken and written varieties. This model, or something close to it, has been echoed by numerous other literacy theorists and researchers, including Olson (1977); Britton, Burgess, Martin, McLeod, and Rosen (1975); Bereiter and Scardamalia (1982); Shuy (1987); and Colombi (2002).

Vygotsky's (1986) theory of cognitive development also places speech at the core of learning to write. The important contribution of the Vygotskian model is the essential role it gives to social interaction in the development of a learner's higher cognitive skills, specifically reading and writing. Again, this view is not unique to Vygotsky (see, e.g., Clay, 1991; Holdaway, 1984); there is general agreement among applied linguists and composition theorists that children learn to read and write based on their prior knowledge of spoken language and on their experiences with social interaction (Dickinson, Wolf, & Stotsky, 1993; Zebroski, 1994).

However, having become acquainted with Francisco, Oscar, and Manuela, we can see that the assumptions that inform writing pedagogy for L1 learners do not always hold up when applied to older students learning to write in their second language. Both the differentiation model and Vygotskian theory are naturalistic approaches; that is, they assume **a natural progression** from speaking to writing, since that is what occurs with children learning a first language. What creates theoretical difficulties for L2 practitioners, especially for those who work with adult learners, are cases like Oscar's, where L2 writing skills are developed and refined without a strong basis in the spoken language. Clearly, L2 learners, and L2 adult learners in particular, present a more complicated and varied picture of literacy development than do L1 children. This seems only reasonable, given the wide variety of educational backgrounds and life experiences that older learners bring to their encounters with L2 writing.

What is needed then is a model for L2 writing development, that takes into account this diversity of learners and developmental phenomena. The three case studies described here suggest that there exists a **continuum of modality preferences,** rather than a stage model, where learners range along a continuum according to their preferences for writing or for speech as the primary vehicle for SLA (see Figure 6; Weissberg, 2000). In terms of modality preference, a given learner may display a symmetrical acquisition style, like Manuela, or an asymmetrical style, like Oscar and Francisco. In the former case, the learner uses both spoken and written modalities to drive the acquisition process forward, adding new lexical and syntactic items in one modality and readily transferring them to the other. In the latter case, learners tend to give preference to one modality over the other as the primary engine for their uptake of new linguistic items. The items acquired in the preferred modality are transferred to the weaker one only after a time lag, if at all. In some cases, like Oscar's, the weaker modality (in his case, speech) may stagnate and fall further behind as the stronger one surges ahead.

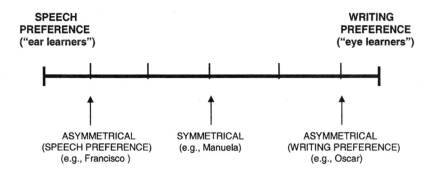

Figure 6. A modality preference model for acquisition of L2 writing. (Reprinted from "Developmental Relationships in the Acquisition of English Syntax: Writing vs. Speech," by R. Weissberg, 2000, *Learning and Instruction, 10,* p. 49. With permission of Elsevier.)

It is tempting to assume that international students with strong academic backgrounds in their home countries tend to have an asymmetrical preference for writing as their primary acquisition tool, while immigrant or Generation 1.5 (Harklau, Losey, & Siegal, 1999) students will show a bias toward speech. However, to categorize certain learner groups a priori as speech-preferring or writing-preferring is reductionist. An L2 writer's modality preference cannot be predicted on the basis of his or her immigration history. The notion that all international students are necessarily "eye" learners while U.S.-resident ESL students are "ear" learners would have categorized all three of the ESL writers described in this chapter as preferring the written mode. The actual situation is obviously more complicated. Learners may rely on one modality more than the other in part because of their earlier language experiences and in part because of their particular learning styles. And, the same learner may rely on *both* speech *and* writing at different times and under different circumstances to drive the SLA process forward.

Ultimately, the question of which modality an L2 learner comes to favor for acquisition purposes may be no more than one of settling for the path of least resistance. A learner may prefer one modality over the other simply because he or she has had a developmental head start in it. It thus acts as the **default modality**—that is, the one the learner usually relies on to support and strengthen the weaker modality. This is the case with naturalistic L2 literacy development, where speech is primary, familiar, and therefore easier. The early writing of these learners sounds like their spoken language because it is essentially "speech written down." However, L2 learners like Oscar, who spend most of their social time with L1 friends and family and who have very limited conversational contact with native speakers of the L2, are more likely to rely on their literacy knowledge for L2 development. When such learners are already expert writers in their L1, as Oscar almost certainly was, their expertise in writing makes it an easier and less stressful vehicle than speech for SLA. It thus becomes their modality of choice, and throughout their L2 writing development they may never produce texts with the chatty, informal qualities of speech.

The concept of modality preference is useful in helping writing instructors to appreciate the range of differences that exists among L2 learners and the variety of paths they may take toward acquiring proficiency in writing. How might these insights be used in designing instruction? The next section will examine how the dialogic model of L2 writing instruction accommodates these differences, and how writing teachers can adjust their instruction to account for differences in modality preference among the L2 writers in their classes.

Talk-Write Tasks

As noted at the end of Chapter 2, implementing the dialogic model requires that writing teachers employ a deliberate strategy of injecting conversation opportunities into their instruction at appropriate points. Similarly, accommodating learners' modality preferences requires conscious selection, planning, and sequencing of instructional tasks. The essence of this strategy is to include learning tasks that cater to students on both ends of the modality preference scale. In some tasks, speech functions as the "leading activity" (Zebroski, 1994, p. 157). That is, the conversation subtask is sequenced first in order to push students' writing forward; in other tasks, reading and/or writing tasks are sequenced first, leading to more sophisticated and demanding conversational output. We will use here the general term "talk-write" (Wixon & Stone, 1977; Zoellner, 1969) to refer to both types of tasks, while acknowledging that the term is broad enough to include "write-talk" as well as "write-talk-write" sequences.

Recognition Tasks

Practice in recognizing and comparing the features of spoken and written varieties of the second language helps naturalistic, speech-preferring L2 writers begin the process of differentiation (see Figure 1). A few of these features are presented for English in this chart:

Some Differences between Spoken and Written Language (Adapted from Nunan, 1999)	
CONVERSATIONAL SPEECH	**ACADEMIC WRITING**
context dependent	context independent
more personalized	depersonalized
spontaneous, sometimes inaccurate	planned, edited
emphasis on action verbs	emphasis on nouns and nominalization
clauses and fragments linked by coordination	full clauses linked by subordination and embedding
grammatically intricate	lexically dense

Students can see these features in context when they are shown two texts on the same topic side by side, one transcribed from speech, the other written as an academic text. For example, in an ESL writing course for international graduate students, students might compare a written transcript of a professor describing her professional background in conversation with a copy of the same professor's written biodata statement. With the instructor's help, students can identify the lexical, syntactic, and rhetorical differences between the spoken and written versions. Similar recognition exercises can be designed for learners of various ages and proficiency levels (Kantor & Rubin, 1981; Vann, 1981).

Style-Shift Tasks

Style-shift tasks help students become sensitive to stylistic differences in the L2 by asking them to transform a text from casual to careful style, or vice versa. An interesting style-shift exercise is suggested by Reid (1994), who shows students how a topic in biology can be rewritten in three alternative styles, one for elementary school children, another for high school students, and a third for college students. Students are then asked to write three similar paragraphs on a topic in their own areas of expertise. Another kind of style-shift task is suggested by Kantor and Rubin (1981), who describe an exercise in which students write a letter on the same topic to two different audiences, one speech-like—chatty and familiar (to a classmate or friend, for instance)—and the other formal and reserved (to a newspaper editor or a city official). Clay (1991) and Blanton (1992) offer additional style-shift tasks.

Mixed Modality Tasks

Mixed modality tasks help students transfer skills from their stronger modality to their weaker one by sequencing speaking and writing subtasks in a particular order. For example, a mixed modality summary task can be sequenced so that students first read an article, discuss it in a small group, and then write individual summaries. The discussion segment helps learners with a speech preference to internalize vocabulary, phrases, and idea sequences through conversation before they attempt to produce a written text. Similar mixed modality tasks include *dicto-comps* (as in Sadiqa's activity described at the beginning of Chapter 2), conducting an oral interview and then summarizing it in writing (Scane, Guy, & Wenstrom, 1994), and *collaborative drafting,* in which a small work group plans and writes together to produce a joint text (Hirvela, 1999). These tasks all involve a speech-to-writing sequence that caters to speech-dominant learners.

Learners with a modality preference for writing can be helped to strengthen their spoken language by adjusting the sequence of tasks. Some interesting suggestions come from L1 writing classrooms. For example, students can converse in writing with other classmates about an upcoming assignment (via e-mail, for example) before meeting for a group discussion. Or they can present preliminary "dialogue papers" to a small group of peer writers for feedback suggestions before beginning a written essay (Stock & Robinson, 1990).

Donald Rubin and William Dodd (1987) suggest an interesting mixed modality task called "topic sculpting," which sequences a planning phase followed by a speaking phase followed in turn by writing. After selecting their individual topics, students are given private time to think about the topic and identify what they consider to be their "unique perspective" on it (Rubin & Dodd, 1987, p. 38). Then they present their thoughts in a five-minute, semiformal talk to the rest of the group. The oral portion of the task is followed by outlining the topic on paper, which is later developed into a written essay.

From the point of view of modality preferences, topic sculpting offers security and challenges for both writing-dominant and speech-dominant L2 writers. For learners with a modality preference for speech, the oral presentation is a chance to formulate their ideas fluently and in public. For writing-dominant learners, topic sculpting provides needed practice in oral fluency, while the initial planning time allows them to organize their thoughts coherently in advance, an aspect of the task that is likely to be more familiar and comfortable.

Ormand Loomis (2003) describes another interesting mixed modality task that he calls "Tell, tape, transcribe, and transform." Here, each student first tells a personal narrative to a small group of classmates. The narratives are audio-taped as they are being presented. Later, students transcribe their own oral narratives as precisely as they can. Finally, they transform the transcriptions into formal essays.

Conversational Coherence in Writing

In an article provocatively titled "The Shifting Relationships between Speech and Writing," Peter Elbow (1985) notes "how writing of the very highest quality—writing as good as any of us could possibly hope to achieve—not only can but should have many of the essential qualities...inherent in speech" (p. 291). One of these essential qualities is **coherence.** In face-to-face conversation, speakers are under pressure to create meaningful messages that have an immediate, communicative impact (or effect) on their listeners, even if the message itself is not always grammatically well formed. As speakers interact, and as each one tries to make a persuasive case to the other, a natural coherence develops both between and within their utterances.

A positive outcome of talk-write tasks is that this **natural coherence of conversation** sometimes carries over from the speaking subtask into students' writing. The quality of conversational coherence can sometimes be detected in the writing of students who have earlier engaged in conversational tasks about the same topic, especially when it is one that provokes a high level of personal or emotional involvement. The following is a sample of one of Manuela's "quick responses"—an impromptu, in-class writing task that immediately followed a class discussion in which students were asked to critique the ESL writing course:

In my opinion, the academic writing class has helped me a lot in improving my writing skills. I think the course is well orientated to the objective of making strong the writing skills. However, I think this kind of class might be less theoretical and what really we need is more practice. Probably, the homework must be more exigent and, in my opinion, we need more "pressure" in order to push ourselves to improve. Finally, although recognizing that the professor is always looking for fulfilling students' needs, sometimes the organization of the course is a little chaotic because there were too many changes in the syllabus and sometimes the students got a little lost.

Manuela's writing exhibits a logical sequence of ideas signaled by transition expressions, a common text feature of written English. Within the individual sentences, however, there are several examples of personal involvement and of syntactic coordination, both more typical of spoken English. Also speech-like are Manuela's use of noun clauses like *what really we need is...* and verb phrases like *got a little lost* and *helped me a lot*. The expressive vitality and coherence of the response clearly communicate Manuela's message—a diplomatically mixed bag of praise and criticism of the instructor's course.

James Zebroski (1994) and Gordon Wells (2000) have noted a similar phenomenon in students' spontaneous, unplanned writing activities. Such tasks seem to release in writers the speech-like impulse to communicate well on the first attempt, resulting in unusually coherent texts. The same communicative quality has been noted in dialogue journal writing (Weissberg, 1998), where the talk-like writing task directed to a familiar audience about topics of great personal significance to the writer can produce higher-than-usual levels of both coherence and accuracy. (See Chapter 6 for a full discussion of "hybrid" types of writing, such as journaling.)

Conclusion

This chapter has focused on individual differences in the ways L2 learners develop their writing skills. In contrast to theoretical models that posit a universal developmental process from speech to writing, or a strict dichotomy of "eye" versus "ear" learners, we noted that L2 learners do not follow predictable paths to proficiency in writing. We saw clear evidence of these learner differences in the portraits of three international ESL students. We then proposed a modality preference model that attempts to capture this range of differences. We continued with a survey of classroom writing techniques generically termed "talk-write," designed to accommodate the different learning styles of L2 writers as suggested by the preference model. Finally it was noted that talk-write tasks have the additional benefit of helping L2 writers develop a level of coherence in their writing approaching that of natural conversation.

It is appropriate to close this discussion by reemphasizing a cautionary reminder that others, notably Leki (1992) and Reid (1998), have made previously: *L2 writers cannot be categorized as a homogeneous group;* we should not assume the individual differences that distinguish one L2 writer from another to be any less than those that distinguish L1 writers. If anything, L2 writers represent an even more heterogeneous pool of learners, and instructors should consider those differences when planning and executing their writing lessons. As will be seen in subsequent chapters, a dialogic approach to teaching writing gives us a useful perspective from which to create suitable classroom tasks for different L2 writers.

Suggested Tasks

1. Identify the range of **modality preferences** among a small group of L2 writers. Which ones seem to be using their knowledge of the spoken language as a basis for their L2 writing? Which ones appear to be relying on their literacy knowledge? Are there learners in your group who seem to be relying on both?

2. In order to accomplish Task 1, design a technique for **gathering L2 speech and writing data** from a group of L2 writers. What kinds of spoken/written data will you collect? How will you collect it? How frequently will you collect it?

3. Design a method to **analyze and categorize the spoken and written data** collected. What textual features of language will you look at? How will you identify these features? How will you categorize and quantify your findings?

4. To supplement the L2 data you gathered in Task 2, find out as much as you can about the **literacy histories** of your group of L2 writers. What kind of research instrument(s) would you design to accomplish this?

Chapter 4

Beyond Teacher-Talk: Instructional Conversations in the Writing Classroom

"To most truly teach, one must converse; to truly converse is to teach."
(Tharp & Gallimore, 1988, p. 111)

In an intermediate ESL writing class, the teacher is at the board acting as the class secretary while the students contribute words, phrases, and sentences for a group composition. They are writing a one-paragraph summary of an article on solar energy they have already read and discussed. Suggestions for the summary come from nearly every member of the class; the teacher selects those that seem to fit best with the sentences that have already been written and adds them to the paragraph slowly taking shape on the board. Here is a bit of the classroom dialogue that accompanies this activity:

Example 1

T:	Ok, what are we gonna talk about next?
S1:	"The sun provides…"
T:	"…provides" [writes on board]
S1:	"…heat and light"
S2:	"One minute of solar energy is sufficient to supply the daily necessities of…"
S3:	We can use "for example"? "For example, one minute…"

T: Let's put the sentence on the board and see if we can use "for example." I don't know if that's good or not. [writes] "For example, one minute of solar energy..."

S2: "...is sufficient to supply..."

T: "...is enough..." [writes]

S2: "...to supply the daily necessities..."

T: "...the daily needs..."

S2: "needs"?

T: Yeah, that's shorter. The summary's gonna be short, right?

S2: "...of one country..."

T: "...the daily needs..." The daily needs of what? What kind of needs?

S3: Energy.

T: Energy needs. "...the daily energy needs..." [writes] "...of one country"? I don't think that's true. Is that true?

S4: Yes, one country.

T: Let me check. [refers to text book] One country.

S1: The problem is a big amount of this energy is reflected in the space.

S2: Ninety percent.

T: [reading aloud the paragraph on the board] "Ninety percent of the energy is reflected back into space, but one minute of the remaining ten percent is sufficient, or enough, to supply the energy needs of one country." If this was my paragraph, I would find this a little bit difficult because I mean, think about it. Are all countries the same? Do all countries have the same energy needs?

S3: Ah, it depends on how the country is prepared to receive the solar energy.

T: Yeah, and also the requirements of a country, because not all countries have the same energy requirements, so this is really a very simple...this is really an over-generalization. If you were writing this in an essay, I would put in the margin, "Are you sure?" [laughter]

S5: The sentence is not applica...applic...in all the countries of the world.

T: Exactly, that's right. It doesn't apply in general. How can we fix it then?

Reprinted from "Speaking of Writing: Some Functions of Talk in the ESL Composition Class," by R. Weissberg, 1994, *Journal of Second Language Writing, 3,* p. 137. With permission of Elsevier.

This excerpt sounds a bit different from traditional classroom discourse. In fact, it sounds more like conversation than teaching. Of course the collaborative nature of the task has something to do with it, but there are also specific features of the teacher's talk that help to create the free-flowing give-and-take. What are these elements? How do writing teachers create opportunities for them to occur in their classroom discourse, and what do they contribute to the development of L2 learners' writing skills?

As noted in Chapter 2, having L2 writers work in peer groups and in pairs is one way of injecting dialogue into the class routine, and the conversations that occur in these settings help students make useful connections between spoken and written language. This chapter examines the possibility of adapting this kind of dialogic talk to whole-class instruction. The rationale laid out in Chapters 1 and 2 for creating a dialogic atmosphere in the writing class is briefly reviewed, followed by what applied linguists have found out about classroom discourse in general and teacher-talk in particular. Those findings are then interpreted from the perspective of the dialogic model of L2 writing instruction that has been developing. Finally, specific dialogic techniques that teachers of L2 writers can apply to their classroom discourse style, and some general guidelines for facilitating dialogue during whole-class writing instruction, will be explored.

The Rationale for Instructional Dialogue

The problem of implementing the dialogic model in the writing classroom is essentially one of bringing selected features of social conversation to bear on the task of classroom teaching and learning without losing the economy of whole-class instruction. For obvious reasons, one-to-one and small-group conversation cannot replace the classroom lecture or whole-class learning activities, and there are certainly critical moments in classroom writing instruction when dialogue is counterproductive—for example, when it occurs as off-task behavior or when it interferes with the completion of a writing task.

On the other hand, dialogue can be used by teachers and students as a way of breaking through the routinized patterns of traditional classroom lessons, allowing for new patterns of participation and knowledge construction to emerge. As shown in the following section, this is a worthwhile goal for teachers of L2 writers to pursue.

Ever since Socrates introduced the young men of Athens to his interrogational style of instruction, teachers have recognized that students who engage actively in their own learning are better able to accommodate and assimilate new knowledge (Goldenberg, 1993; Nystrand & Gamoran, 1991; Tharp & Gallimore, 1988). This awareness has led language educators to develop the inquiry method (Wells & Chang-Wells, 1992) and collaborative approaches (Bruffee, 1999) to teaching and learning and to promote students' active oral participation in lessons (Barnes, 1990).

In L2 instruction, the argument for active student participation is especially persuasive. In her critique of the comprehension approach to language teaching (the notion that second languages are acquired primarily through the learner's exposure to comprehensible input—listening and reading—rather than through speaking and writing), Merrill Swain (1985) pointed out three benefits for L2 students when they actively participate in oral discourse in class. First, talking helps learners to notice the language structures they are using; that is, talk serves a **consciousness-raising function** for language learners. Second, talking gives learners the opportunity to experiment with new grammatical structures and vocabulary as they communicate and to get feedback from their co-conversationalists on how well those new items work in real-life communication; that is, learners' talk has a **hypothesis-testing function.** Third, by noticing and experimenting out loud with new items in the language, learners train themselves to think analytically about the language forms they are learning. In other words, talking has a **metalinguistic function** for language learners (Swain, 1985).

Most important for L2 learners in a formal classroom setting, the use of conversational dialogue helps them to develop **communicative competence.** In the sheltered environment of the classroom, L2 students learn to make appropriate contributions to the ongoing conversations; they learn how to start conversations and how to end them, how to gain and hold the floor, and how to repair conversations when they break down (Boyd & Maloof, 2000). None of this is possible without their active oral participation. In sum, while comprehension may be necessary for language learning to take place, it is not sufficient for the development of active L2 proficiency. The road to proficiency runs through the territory of social interaction.

The importance of oral practice for second and foreign language learners is well accepted and by now seems self-evident. Less obvious are the roles that classroom conversation plays for L2 learners when the focus of instruction is on writing. L2 writers can benefit from a conversational style of instruction in several ways. First, as we saw in Chapter 1, speech is **developmentally related to writing** (Dickinson, Wolf, & Stotsky, 1993). Just as L1 writers tap their knowledge of the spoken language when they write, L2 writers can also draw upon the linguistic resources of their conversational speech (Sperling & Freedman, 2001). Words, grammatical structures, and turns of phrase all come more easily for writers if they are already present in their oral language and if they are encouraged to use them when writing. And non-native writers who have a strong oral basis in the language can use it not just to increase their fluency in writing but also to help "grow" their underlying L2 proficiency (Harklau, 2002; Reichelt, 1999; Weissberg, 2000).

A second benefit of conversational instruction in the writing classroom is that students with experience in talking about their writing tend to write with **greater coherence** (Nystrand, 1997). By making extended oral contributions to class discussions and by learning to link their contributions to those of others in the conversation, L2 writers develop a sense of "intertextuality" (Boyd & Maloof, 2000, p. 166). That is, they learn to fit their own contributions into the ongoing classroom discussion—confirming, extending, contradicting, or simply responding to the contributions of others. This is a transferable skill; writers who can sense the direction of the ongoing conversation and who can carve out their own role in it are better able to anticipate their readers' needs and to meet them through the texts they write.

Third, teachers who teach writing conversationally are modeling for their students the reality of writing as **a meaningful, socially situated activity,** not as an isolated set of artificial exercises cordoned off from the rest of their lives. Teachers can also model for their students the thought processes and problem-solving strategies that writers use when they compose text. For example, in the classroom dialogue presented on pages 50–52, we "heard" the instructor thinking out loud about a variety of composing issues—invention problems *(what are we gonna talk about next?)*, making sentences clear *(. . ."daily needs". . .The daily needs of what? What kind of needs?)*, and revising *(If this was my paragraph, I would find this a little bit difficult because I mean, think about it. Are all countries the same?. . .It [the sentence in the text] doesn't apply in general. How can we fix it then?)*. The topic of modeling will be explored later in this chapter.

In connection with the social context of writing, recall Vygotsky's (1986) argument that all higher cognitive processing develops out of social interaction. This means that the kind of thinking out loud demonstrated by the writing teacher in the example that opened this chapter can be internalized by students for their own use in their later writing. The implication is that teacher-directed conversation in the writing class is not supplemental to instruction; *it is the very core of the instruction itself.* As Wells and Chang-Wells (1992) claim, "In a very important sense, education *is* dialog" (p. 32).

The rationale presented here applies to both native and non-native learners: If thought is social interaction internalized and if writing is the outcome of thinking processes, then a writing class without conversation is a class stripped of an essential feature of effective teaching. With this rationale in mind, now consider how the dialogic model for whole-class instruction fits into the broad range of discourse styles found in language classrooms.

Patterns of Classroom Talk

Teachers, even experienced ones, are often unconscious of the patterns of oral discourse that they establish and perpetuate while teaching (Cazden, 1988). It can be unsettling for teachers to discover through an audio- or video-tape recording of their classes the extent to which they monopolize classroom talk, how often they predetermine their students' responses, or the fact that they control classroom exchanges so tightly that students have little opportunity to engage in meaningful dialogue. However, once teachers become sensitized to the discourse character of their classes, they are in a position to adjust it. Some of the patterns of instructional talk that discourse analysts have identified in L1 and L2 classrooms, and how those patterns can affect the quality of writing instruction, are shown.

Teaching as Transmission: The IRE Sequence

Teachers typically produce not only the great majority of talk that takes place in classrooms (Flanders, 1970; Nystrand, 1997), but also organize classroom discourse into tightly controlled patterns. The most recognized of these is what is known as the IRE sequence (Mehan, 1985), a three-move cycle begin-ning with the teacher's **initiation** ("I"—usually a question to which he or she already knows the answer), followed by a student's **response** ("R"), and terminating with the teacher's **evaluative** comment ("E"). Mehan's classic example of the IRE sequence shows a teacher and a student engaged in the following exchange:

Example 2

T: What time is it, Denise? (I)
S: Two-thirty. (R)
T: Very good, Denise! (E)

(from Mehan, 1985, p. 126)

Mehan demonstrates how typical lessons are built up of repeated cycles of the IRE pattern, resulting in an overall 2:1 ratio of teacher turns to student turns. Two other important facts about IRE teaching should be noted: Not only do the teacher's moves outnumber the students' moves, but they are also usually much longer. Second, the "R" move allows for little or no cognitive or communicative effort on the student's part other than recall; it is a predetermined response to a question the teacher already knows the answer to. It is not surprising then that IRE sequences are seldom encountered in discourse situations outside the classroom—they are by nature one-sided and non-dialogic.

The IRE pattern typifies **transmission style** teaching (Barnes, 1990; Nystrand, 1997; Onore, 1990)—the pedagogical assump-tion that classroom learning is a one-way transfer of knowledge from teacher to student. In Cynthia Onore's (1990) words, in this style of teaching, "Learning is a process of reproducing the contours of the teacher's thinking, knowledge is a commodity consisting of single, correct answers and the teacher is the sole transmitter and evaluator of learning" (p. 59). However, other studies of teacher talk and classroom discourse indicate that some teachers hold a quite different view of what it means to teach. The difference is apparent in the variety of discourse patterns they use to structure their classroom talk.

Alternative Styles of Teacher Talk

If the IRE sequence and the transmission style model are the common currency of classroom teaching (and recent research in education seems to indicate that they still are—see Boyd & Maloof, 2000; Nystrand, 1997; Wells, 2000)—there are other models in use by teachers who have moved away from lock-step classroom discourse patterns (Wells, 1990, 1993). In fact, there appears to be a continuum of classroom discourse styles in use by writing teachers, ranging from the traditional transmission style on one end to a conversational style on the other (Gutierrez, 1994; Nystrand & Gamoran, 1991).

From her observation of ESL writing classes in elementary and middle schools, Kris Gutierrez (1994) identified three points along this classroom discourse continuum and labeled them **Recitation, Responsive,** and **Responsive/Collaborative** (see Figure 7). Each point on the continuum represents a *script,* an unwritten and perhaps unconscious view on the teacher's part of what constitutes appropriate verbal behavior in a classroom lesson. Scripts appear to the observer as "recurring patterns of [language] activity with and across events in a classroom that...are stable ways of engaging with others" (Gutierrez, 1994, p. 341). In the *recitation script,* for example, the teacher controls the oral discourse of the class by using the IRE question-response-evaluation pattern, thus reserving the right to select who will speak and when, and determining all or most of the topics of discussion raised during a lesson. The recitation script might be taken as the outward manifestation of the notion that there is only one correct answer to each question—i.e., the answer that the teacher has in mind (Gutierrez, 1994, p. 343).

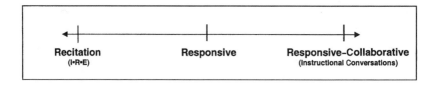

Figure 7. A continuum of classroom discourse scripts (after Gutierrez, 1994, and Nystrand & Gamoran, 1991).

Further along the discourse continuum lies the *responsive script*—a more relaxed variant of the IRE pattern with more opportunities for a greater number of students to respond to a teacher's question, some self-selection by student speakers, and some acceptance by the teacher of student-generated topics. The overall atmosphere in a classroom dominated by the responsive script is still one where students try to come up with the teacher's desired answer but where they reach it in a more egalitarian, cooperative way. An important feature of the responsive script is what Gordon Wells (1993) has called the IRF sequence, in which the last of the three turns in the sequence is a "follow-up" rather than an "evaluation." The critical point in substituting "F" for "E" is that teachers always have the discretion to use the final move in the three-move cycle as an opportunity to "extend the student's answer, draw out its significance or to make connections with other parts of the students' total experience," rather than simply to evaluate the student's previous response (p. 30). This pattern is shown in the following excerpt from the first example on pages 51–52:

T: If this was my paragraph, I would find this a little bit difficult because I mean, think about it. Are all countries the same? Do all countries have the same energy needs? (I)

S3: Ah, it depends on how the country is prepared to receive the solar energy. (R)

T: Yeah, and also the requirements of a country, because not all countries have the same requirements, so this is really a very simple...this is really an overgeneralization... (F)

S5: The sentence is not applica...applic...in all the countries of the world. (R)

T: Exactly, that's right. It doesn't apply in general. How can we fix it then? (E + F + I)

With its combination of teacher control and students' freedom to make substantive contributions, the responsive script is an effective way for writing teachers to manage open-ended discussions while moving toward a specific lesson objective (Cumming, 1992; Weissberg, 1994).

At the opposite end of the continuum from recitation is the *responsive-collaborative script.* In this pattern the teacher still controls the learning agenda and is still responsible for structuring classroom talk, but students are allowed to build on each other's previous utterances with less intrusion from the teacher. The teacher asks fewer known-answer questions and more authentic ones—those for which there is no pre-determined answer. The teacher also actively acknowledges the students' oral contributions and incorporates them into the ongoing conversation. In the responsive/collaborative script there is still a bias toward students getting the "correct" information, but the general atmosphere is one of an evolving, extended group conversation, guided by the teacher and incorporating contributions from as many students in the class as possible. Nystrand (1997) provides the following example of the Responsive/Collaborative script from a lesson in a high school literature class:

Example 3

Teacher (at the board):	I had a lot of trouble getting everything down [on the board], and I think I missed the part about trying to boycott...Did I get everything down, John?
John:	What about the guy who didn't really think these kids were a pest?
Teacher:	Yeah, okay. What's his name? Do you remember?
Alicia:	Wasn't it Turner?
Teacher:	Was it Turner?
Several students:	Yes.
Teacher:	Okay, so Mr. Turner resisted white help. Why? Why would he want to keep shopping at that terrible store?

John: There was only one store to buy from because all the other ones were white.

Teacher: Well, the Wall store was white too.

Tom: [addressing John] Is it Mr. Holling's store? Is that it?

John: No. Here's the reason. They don't get paid till the cotton comes in. But throughout the year they still have to buy stuff—food, clothes, seed, stuff like that. So the owner of the plantation will sign for what they buy at the store so...they can buy stuff on credit.

Teacher: So [reading aloud from the board] he has to have credit in order to buy things and this store is the only one that will give it to him.

Felice: I was just going to say, it was the closest store.

Teacher: Okay, it's the closest store; it seems to be in the middle of the area; a lot of sharecroppers who don't get paid cash—they get credit at that store...so it's going to be very hard for her to organize that boycott; she needs to exist on credit. Yeah?

[etc.]

(from Nystrand, 1997, pp. 1–2)

Other researchers have referred to this responsive-collaborative script as "exploratory talk" (Boyd & Maloof, 2000), "transactional discourse" (Barnes, 1990), "dialogic instruction" (Wells, 1990), or "contingently responsive teaching" (Wells & Chang-Wells, 1992). Tharp and Gallimore (1988, 1991) have perhaps characterized it best as **instructional conversation**— the topic of the remainder of this chapter.

Instructional Conversations

An instructional conversation (IC) is a natural-sounding teacher-student dialogue with an instructional purpose (Tharp

& Entz, 2003; Tharp & Gallimore, 1988). The special function of ICs is *to embed instruction within social interaction,* and thus they constitute a kind of classroom discourse script that holds much promise for writing teachers seeking to develop a dialogic classroom environment. ICs differ in some important ways from traditional teacher-dominated classroom discourse. First, they do not follow routinized IRE-type patterns and are therefore less predicable, which makes them resemble natural conversation more than conventional teacher talk. Second, ICs are more participatory; that is, more students are able to talk longer than in transmission-style teaching. Third, ICs are inherently dialogic. In building ICs teachers must make a concerted effort to incorporate students' topics, comments, and questions into the developing dialogue rather than focusing solely on their own teaching agenda (Nystrand, 1997).

Teachers construct ICs by providing their student writers with various kinds of verbal assistance. Six kinds of assistance are examined here through dialogue, all of which plays a role in creating instructional conversations.

Turn-Taking

In her studies of classroom language lessons, Courtney Cazden (1988) found that teachers who attended to "speaking rights" (who gets to speak and for how long) created more participatory discussions in their classes. Maureen Boyd and Donald Rubin (2002) also looked at the issue of turn-taking during whole-class instruction and identified what they call a "Student Critical Turn" (SCT). SCTs are extended student talk-turns that are more than short responses to a teacher's question. In an SCT, a student can "restate or question what others had said and/or ... [relate] the topic or issue to their own experiences in order to assist understanding" (Boyd & Rubin, 2002, pp. 520–521). In classroom lessons that follow the recitation script, these types of turns are normally reserved for the teacher. In their study of ESL upper-level elementary school classrooms, Boyd and Rubin found that the number of extended SCTs in a lesson was a key index to students' active participation in classroom discussions.

Allowing Wait-Time

In creating ICs, teachers must attend to patterns of silence as well as talk. Cazden's (1988) analysis of classroom discourse identified wait-time as a critical feature of instructional conversations. In her discourse studies of classroom talk, she found that teachers who gave their students at least three seconds' wait-time to respond to a question before jumping in with their own follow-up ran more effective classroom discussions.

By definition, an IC can't be created if students don't participate. Therefore, the length and number of turns the teacher makes available to student speakers during whole-class discussion and the wait-time she provides for student responses after she asks a question are critical quantifiable elements in the construction of ICs. Other, more qualitative forms of student assistance inherent in ICs are discussed next.

Modeling

Modeling occurs when the teacher "offer[s] behavior for imitation," (Tharp & Gallimore, 1988, p. 47). In the first classroom dialogue example (page 51), the ESL writing instructor transcribed a student's sentence on the board and then critiqued it:

T: "...the daily needs..." The daily needs of what? What kind of needs?

S3:   Energy.

In so doing, he modeled the writer's act of **reviewing and revising his own text.** Later, in the same excerpt, the teacher opened the textbook and said:

> *T:*   Let me check. [refers to textbook] One country.

Here he was modeling **consultation** as a means of resolving doubts while drafting a text.

In addition to modeling writing processes, teachers can also model a variety of classroom participation roles for their students through dialogue—those of **questioner, clarifier, summarizer, topic initiator,** and **sharer of experience** (Boyd & Maloof, 2000), to name a few. These are speaker roles usually reserved for the teacher in traditional classroom discourse, but because ICs allow students and teachers to break away from the repetitive IRE cycles of the recitation script, students have the freedom to experiment with a greater variety of roles.

Feeding-Back

Another form of verbal assistance that distinguishes ICs from more traditional discourse scripts is **feeding-back,** a dialogic way of guiding students away from errors and toward enhanced understanding and performance. Feedback is built into the last step of the IRE cycle; however, feeding-back in the context of an IC is qualitatively different since it is embedded in dialogue. The following example from an advanced ESL technical writing class shows the writing teacher using dialogic feedback to help her students understand the technical definition of a common term:

Example 4

> *T:*   As we're using the word "illustration" here, what does it refer to? Look back at your notes if you need to. What does illustration mean?

S1: Figure? Table?

T: OK, those are examples. An illustration is in words. What did we say it was?

S2: It explains something.

T: That's its purpose. What part of the research report is it?

S2: Explains the results.

T: Well, yeah. That's its function. OK, somebody said it.

S3: Non-verbal.

T: The non-verbal, or the nontextual part of the research report, and that's what we mean here by illustration....

(from Weissberg, 1994, p. 137)

Rather than directly correcting or evaluating her students (the "E" in IRE), the instructor guides them with dialogic feedback to a new, technical definition for a familiar word.

Responding to students' errors is a critical and complex issue in teaching L2 writers (Ferris, 2002), and one further explored in Chapter 6. The crucial point here is that teachers can provide feedback, like other teaching acts, within a conversational context.

Questioning

Teachers who are sensitive to the discourse scripts of their classrooms are aware of the crucial role that their own questions play. As Tharp and Gallimore (1988) note, "questions in classrooms are most often embedded in the recitation script and are concerned with assessment....Few questions are used in responsive, in-flight discussion" (p. 58). They point out, however, that "questioning is a central [teaching] device, because questions call up the use of language and in this way assist thinking" (p. 59).

Questioning is a key element in all teaching (Socrates' questioning style will be examined in Chapter 7), and as many observers of classroom discourse have noted, all teacher questions are not created equal (Cazden, 1988; Mehan, 1985; Nystrand, 1997). Thus, dialogic teachers who use ICs as their discourse script monitor the kinds of questions they ask during their lessons and then evaluate the types of student responses that their questions elicit. When a teacher asks a student a known-answer question (as in Example 4, *What does* illustration *mean?*), the effect on the ensuing instructional conversation can be quite different from that of an authentic question, like the one in Example 3 (page 60):

Teacher (at the board):	I had a lot of trouble getting everything down [on the board], and I think I missed the part about trying to boycott...Did I get everything down, John?
John:	What about the guy who didn't really think these kids were a pest?

The teacher's authentic question here signals his students that he is genuinely seeking information with their help, not assessing their mastery of lesson content through recitation.

Dialogic teachers choose question types depending on their pedagogical goals at specific points throughout the writing lesson, and how to frame the question becomes a strategic issue. Seen in this light, teacher questioning is not a simple "known-answer questions = bad, authentic questions = good" dichotomy, and known-answer questions can play an important role in creating ICs. As Boyd and Rubin (2002) and Wells (1993) have argued, simply because a question is a known-answer question doesn't necessarily mean that it works against effective classroom conversations. In their study, Boyd and Rubin (2002) found that teachers' known-answer questions often immediately preceded STCs; that is, known-answer questions in certain discourse contexts elicited lengthy, high-quality student contributions. Based on these findings, Boyd and Rubin (2002) make an important distinction between teacher questions that serve to *assist* students and those used to *assess them*. Both known-answer questions and authentic questions can be assistive if they result in extended classroom dialogue. For example, when a teacher is reviewing material with the class from a previous day's lesson, closed-ended, known-answer questions may be more appropriate. However, during class brainstorming sessions, open-ended authentic questions are likely to work better.

Uptake

Another way that teachers provide dialogic assistance is by practicing **uptake** (Nystrand, 1997; Nystrand & Gamoran, 1991). Uptake occurs when a teacher deliberately incorporates elements of a student's previous response into her own talk, as shown in the following excerpt:

> *T:* What is the other kind of narrator?
> *S:* **Third-person narrator**.
> *T:* Well, yeah, **third-person narrator**. And what is that called? Somebody's whispering the word.
> *S:* **Omniscient** narrator.
> *T:* What do you mean by **"omniscient"**?
> (etc.)

(from Nystrand, 1997, p. 83, boldface added)

Uptake can be accomplished with known-answer questions, authentic questions, or with a combined statement-plus-question, as in this excerpt. It is more likely to occur when the teacher consciously links her own talk thematically and linguistically to the previous contributions of her students (Tannen, 1985). Forging links between student talk and her own requires the teacher to listen actively and to watch for opportunities to use her students' contributions to move the class toward a teaching point (Boyd & Maloof, 2000).

Teachers who are adept at practicing uptake "weave" their students' contributions into the ongoing oral tapestry of instruction (Boyd & Rubin, 2002; Wells, 1990). By including pieces of their students' previous comments in their questions, they ensure that students' comments become part of the fabric of the lesson. And when they incorporate words and phrases from their students' earlier responses, they indicate that they take their students' talk seriously—that it counts for knowledge and that it is worthy of being part of the lesson. Thus, teachers who practice uptake as part of their discourse style help students become legitimate participants in the instructional conversation.

Cognitive Structuring

A final feature of instructional conversations identified by Tharp and Gallimore is what they call "cognitive structuring." In cognitive structuring, the teacher makes statements that give students a new cognitive framework, a new insight, or an alternative way to think about a problem. When the teacher in Example 1 (page 51) suggests a different lexical choice and then follows up with a general point about summaries:

S2:   "...to supply the daily necessities..."

T: "...the daily needs..."

S2:   "needs"?

T: Yeah, that's shorter. The summary's gonna be short, right?

he is promoting cognitive structuring. The teacher in Example 3 (page 61) does the same when he responds to a student with an instructional point piggybacked on her remark:

Felice: I was just going to say, it was the closest store.

   T: Okay, it's the closest store; it seems to be in the middle of the area; a lot of sharecroppers who don't get paid cash—they get credit at that store... so it's going to be very hard for her to organize that boycott; she needs to exist on credit. Yeah?

Teachers also engage in cognitive structuring when they make summary statements at the end of an instructional conversation segment or when they offer a new idea to push the class conversation along.

Cognitive structuring differs from transmission-style teaching. It is an instructional act built on the give-and-take classroom conversation. Like modeling, questioning, and feeding-back, cognitive structuring must be viewed dialogically to appreciate how it contributes to creating ICs and how it differs from lecturing. New information imparted to students during an extended classroom lecture does not qualify as cognitive structuring because it is not embedded in a conversational context.

For L2 writers, it is the **cognitive consequences** of social interaction that make the qualitative difference between lessons built around instructional conversations and those run according to the recitation script. As shown in this chapter, ICs infuse classroom lessons with a mix of modeling, questioning, feeding-back, uptake, and instructing, producing "a lively and cooperative teacher-learner interaction" (Tharp & Gallimore, 1988, p. 57). When L2 learners participate in this rich discursive mix, they engage with lesson material at a deeper cognitive level than in lessons scripted as recitation (Ellis, 1999). They learn to propose, debate, and critique ideas and language issues with the instructor, with each other, and with the texts they write. They learn to question assumptions, to extend and elaborate ideas, to initiate and change topics, and to restate and clarify ideas. When it is enriched by instructional conversations, the writing classroom becomes a site for academic apprenticeship, where L2 writers learn to analyze critically the strengths and weaknesses of the arguments they hear, those they read, and those they write—where they learn, in short, to be academic writers.

Creating ICs: Some General Strategies and Guidelines

Clearly, teachers of L2 writers who are serious about helping their students master school writing must also be serious about the oral discourse in their classroom lessons. Just as clearly, dialogic writing classrooms don't come about simply through the fortuitous combination of a particular teacher and a particular group of gregarious students. They grow out of teachers' deliberate efforts to provide assistance to their student writers by creating instructional conversations as a primary characteristic of their teaching style. Although ICs may come more naturally to some writing teachers than to others, all teachers can learn to incorporate them into their whole-class teaching.

Some specific features of instructional conversations have been examined; however, not all the factors that help to create ICs are linguistic or discourse features of teacher talk. Some come into play even before classroom instruction begins. Three of them will be discussed here.

Content-Based Writing Curricula

A content-based course plan supports the writing teacher's efforts to create instructional conversations during whole-class instruction. This is because a content base provides L2 writers with an integrated, meaningful foundation of ideas to talk, argue, and write about. Students in content-based writing courses are better able to engage in quality classroom discussions than those in skill-based courses because they deal in-depth with sustained themes, gaining familiarity and expertise with the content over time. For example, non-native students in a college writing course who spend a semester writing about a set of related issues can discuss and write about those issues with greater language facility and control than if their writing and reading assignments during the course jump from one unrelated topic to another (Weissberg & Lipoufski, 2002). And, if the course content deals with themes of personal interest and meaning to students, there will likely be even more occasions for extended class discussions.

Engaging Materials

To provide meaningful content as the foundation for dialogue and discussion, teachers should examine possible textbooks, reading selections, and other course materials with the goal of the dialogic classroom explicitly in mind. Course materials should not only be thematically connected but also engaging and relevant to L2 writers' interests and life experiences. The writing topics and reading selections presented by the authors of commercial composition textbooks don't always satisfy these conditions, so instructors practicing the dialogic approach may choose to replace or supplement an adopted textbook with their own, or student-found, materials. Thematically linked articles from local news sources about issues that students care about serve as springboards for instructional conversations in class and subsequent writing assignments (Weissberg & Lipoufski, 2002).

Group Work vs. Whole Class Instruction

Obviously, collaborative writing projects for groups of students are more likely to promote dialogue than individual writing tasks. For this reason, dialogic writing teachers often construct their course syllabi to include project-based writing activities in addition to, or instead of, individual assignments. Wells (2002) describes several examples of successful projects, including classes in which book clubs (or "literature circles") provide a forum for student discussion in preparation for a collaborative writing assignment. He also describes an elementary classroom in which a "knowledge wall" was used by students to post ideas for future writing assignments on sticky notes; their ongoing conversation-by-notes created an informal written discussion about the topics proposed. This led to later writing assignments in which students were asked to summarize the essence of the earlier "conversations" posted on the knowledge wall.

In another writing class developed by my graduate student, Lynne Lucero, a group of students in an adult ESL program wrote a series of autobiographical reading selections and related texts, thus creating its own reading-and-composition textbook. In a similar project organized by my student teacher, Jean Baca, a class of EFL tourism students in Central America wrote and illustrated with photos a guidebook for English-speaking visitors to popular tourist sites in their country. In one of my recent university writing classes, groups of students worked with a series of three published articles that I had provided them about social justice issues. They then worked in groups to find one additional article on their own that would fit in with the general theme. In a culminating writing activity, the groups wrote synthesis papers summarizing and commenting on the four articles.

Collaborative projects like these help to promote a dialogic atmosphere in the classroom; however, they do not necessarily create opportunities for ICs. Group talk can in fact degenerate into non-constructive and off-task behavior. ICs, on the other hand, are by definition teacher led and are guided by the teacher's knowledge of the subject matter and expertise at keeping the conversation goal directed and participatory. From the perspective of the dialogue approach to teaching writing, this constitutes a major advantage of whole-class instruction over group work. More will be said about the pluses and minuses of group work in Chapter 7.

Conversations of a Special Kind

One of the leading proponents of the dialogic approach to teaching writing, Martin Nystrand, makes the claim that:

> The extent to which classroom discourse resembles conversation is…an excellent criterion for judging both the instructional quality of the discourse and the extent of substantive student engagement. (Nystrand & Gamoran, 1991, p. 267)

While natural conversation sets the model for whole-class instruction following the responsive/collaborative script, ICs differ from casual, unplanned talk in some important ways. In ICs the teacher keeps a clear (if not always overtly expressed) pedagogical focus throughout the conversation. The focus may shift throughout a lesson—from sentence punctuation to topic development to paragraph organization—and may deviate from the topic from time to time, but the instructional goals are never completely abandoned to the vagaries of casual conversation. The teacher must sometimes bring reluctant students back on topic, may have to ignore one student's comment in favor of another's, or may even indicate that a particular student comment is off the mark. By keeping a loose but consistent rein on the direction of the dialogue, the teacher helps students stay on target and, when necessary, can ratchet up the instructional level to challenge students with new and more difficult topics and tasks (Goldenberg, 1993).

Before experimenting with instructional conversations in their whole-class teaching, it is helpful for writing teachers to first get a sense of the existing discourse patterns in their classes. They can accomplish this by carrying out a **discourse audit.** With students' permission, the teacher first records one or two classroom lessons and then performs an informal discourse analysis on the recordings. Important features to listen for are those covered in this chapter: the distribution, number, and length of turns on both the teacher's and students' sides of the dialogue; the types of questions asked by the teacher and the kinds of student responses that are elicited in each case; the extent to which the teacher practices uptake by incorporating students' oral contributions into the ongoing discourse; the average length of wait-time that the teacher affords students after soliciting a response; the types of writing-related behaviors that the teacher models; the types of oral feedback provided; and how instruction is given, either through cognitive structuring or extended teacher lecturing.

Once their audits are complete, teachers can step back and take a broader perspective of their discourse styles by assigning each recorded lesson to a point on the continuum of discourse scripts shown in Figure 7. The results of the discourse audit will then allow them to make principled judgments about how (or whether) to reorganize the oral discourse in their classes.

Nystrand (1997) points out that "the bottom line for [writing] instruction is that the quality of student learning is closely linked to the quality of classroom talk" (p. 29). If L2 student writers are expected to create coherent texts on paper, they must be provided with a coherent classroom discourse that honors and incorporates their oral contributions.

Suggested Tasks and Discussion Questions

1. Record one or more of your own writing lessons and conduct **a discourse audit** on your oral teaching style. Consider the changes you would make in order to incorporate more instructional conversation into your whole-class teaching style.

2. Observe one of your colleagues or a more senior teacher teaching a writing class and look for signs of instructional conversation in his/her teaching. Try to identify the **particular discourse patterns** of this teacher that appear to promote or inhibit the development of a dialogic teaching style.

3. Consider the discourse style of a favorite professor in a course you are currently taking. What are some **specific elements of his/her style of classroom talk** that make his/her classes so effective and enjoyable?

4. What differences (if any) do you think teachers should make in their classroom discourse styles when they are dealing with **L2 rather than L1 writing students?**

5. Finally, with a view toward Chapter 5, consider this: What important differences would you expect to find between a writing teacher's oral discourse style in whole-class instruction and the oral discourse of a good writing tutor during **one-on-one tutoring?**

Chapter 5

Conversations in the Writing Tutorial

with Gina L. Hochhalter

> *"Nearly everyone who writes likes—and needs—to talk*
> *about his or her writing, preferably to someone who will*
> *really listen… [someone who will] draw them out, ask*
> *them questions they would not think to ask themselves."*
> (from Stephen North, "The Idea of a Writing Center,"
> 1984, pp. 439–440)

Chapter 4 focused on creating dialogue in the writing classroom during whole-class instruction. This chapter is concerned with the kind of talk generated by L2 student writers interacting one-on-one with their instructors or tutors in writing conferences. Conferencing and tutoring are perhaps the most common and potentially valuable supplements to classroom instruction in writing (Sperling, 1991), the first taking place between an instructor and a student, often in the instructor's office, and the second between a tutor and a student client, often in a university writing center or learning laboratory. For our purposes in this chapter, both events will be referred to as tutoring. Our goal will be to see how instructional dialogues are created during tutoring and how this kind of talk can provide support for the L2 student writer.

If, as we have been arguing throughout this book, conversation lies at the heart of writing and learning to write, then the writing tutorial is an ideal setting for putting the oral-writing connection into action and for seeing the effects of dialogic instruction on students' written texts. In fact, applied linguists have been putting together a body of research on L1 and L2 writing conference discourse that looks at precisely these areas (see, e.g., Harris, 1990; Patthey-Chavez & Ferris, 1997; Powers, 1993; Thonus, 1999a, 1999b; Williams, 2002). The next section briefly looks at this research. The remainder of Chapter 5 is devoted to a detailed look at oral scaffolding—the dialogic mechanism by which tutors help novices reach higher levels of writing proficiency. The chapter concludes with some suggestions for training tutors who work with L2 writers.

Research on Tutoring

To get some perspective on the writing tutorial, it's helpful to understand how it has evolved over time in college writing centers, the places where tutoring and tutorial conversations have been most carefully researched. The tutorial was seen initially as a way to serve students who were having "difficulty adapting to the traditional or 'normal' conventions of the college classroom" (Bruffee, 1995, p. 87). The tutor's job was one of normalizing the language of problem writers, meaning that a tutor would focus on what Bakhtin (cited by Gillam, 1991, p. 127) called the "centripetal forces" in language—the standard conventions that centralize, unify, and stabilize written language. These include the grammatical rules, lexical usage, and discourse conventions of formal written language. In writing centers where this concern for standardization took precedence, the tutor's primary job was to "fix" broken pieces of student writing (North, 1984).

Over time, however, the writing center has become a place where collaborative conversations about writing take place between students and their tutors. In today's writing center, what Bakhtin labeled the "centrifugal forces" of language, those that tend to "destabilize language through multiple meanings, varying contexts, and the free play of dialects," are also allowed to come into play (Gillam, 1991, p. 128). The notion that language is by nature dynamic and unstable, while classroom instruction in standard written language has traditionally forced student writers into a straitjacket, has led writing center tutors and their trainers "to view themselves as liberating agents, working to free students from the oppressive, centripetal forces of academic discourse" (p. 128). Tutoring in these centers has changed from a focus on corrective feedback to a "minimalist" activity (Brooks, 1991) in which the tutor takes a hands-off approach to the student's text, playing more the role of a good listener than an instructor. In minimalist tutoring, the student, not the tutor, is responsible for the corrections and revisions to a draft.

Some have criticized the practice of minimalist tutoring as inappropriate for L2 writers. For example, Judith Powers (1993) questioned its effectiveness with ESL writers in her study in which she discovered that the non-directive style of tutoring favored by the minimalists "appeared to fail (or work differently) when applied to ESL conferences" (p. 236). Some of the reasons for the failure were obvious. While tutors can often help their L1 clients become independent editors, able to find and correct their own mechanical errors, this strategy is not as likely to succeed with L2 writers. Instead, Powers suggested that tutors working with L2 writers take on the more directive "role of *informant* rather than collaborator" when conferencing (p. 238, italics added).

Other reasons for adopting a more directive approach are perhaps less obvious. L2 writers (especially international students) may be culturally unprepared to work with a tutor who acts more like a peer than an authority figure. In a study on writing center tutorials with ESL writers, Terese Thonus (1993) found that L2 students tended not to be as involved conversationally with tutors as were their L1 counterparts. She also found that L2 students became frustrated when tutors were reluctant to exercise authority or seemed to shy away from giving students clear directions and correction (Thonus, 1993). For these reasons, she, like Powers, urged tutors to depart from minimalist, hands-off style tutoring (Thonus, 1999b).

This brief review of the research on writing tutorials shows that there has been an evolving view of how tutors should interact with their clients, how they should deal with L2 writers, and how they might resolve the tension between proponents of hands-on versus hand-off tutoring. It appears that what works in writing conferences for L1 writers may not work as well for ESL writers, for whom the centripetal forces—the "norms" of the written language—may be a central concern. The argument seems to boil down to this: Since L2 writers are less likely to be familiar with the range of acceptable alternatives available in written English, they are not as likely to take advantage of the freedom offered by hands-off tutoring. The worst-case scenario is that minimalist tutoring essentially abandons L2 writers to their own devices, leading them to produce written work that simply won't meet the expectations of their course instructors.

From the perspective of the dialogue approach to teaching L2 writers, how are we to interpret the research on writing tutorials? If we accept Vygotsky's theory that social interaction is the necessary precursor to a learner's cognitive development, then we must recognize that these studies, by focusing on the oral discourse of tutorials, are very much on track. Jessica Williams (2002, 2004) clarifies the point still further in her claim that without collaborative conversation, an L2 writer is unlikely to internalize new forms and new writing strategies from the tutorial. Indeed, the Vygotskian perspective helps us appreciate that the success of a tutoring session is in large part a function of the tutor's skill at **embedding instruction in dialogue,** that the tutor's principal job, like the classroom writing teacher's, is to create instructional dialogues with students. The next section takes a closer look at how this is accomplished.

Topics and Functions of Tutor Talk

What do tutors talk about during their sessions with clients? The published research on L2 writing conferences shows that the issues they deal with vary from the smallest points of sentence construction to larger issues of the writing process. Some of these topics are surveyed in this section.

Correcting Grammar

Sentence-level grammar problems are a common focus in tutorials with L2 writers (Aljaafreh & Lantolf, 1994; Myers, 2003; Powers, 1993; Williams, 2002), making up much of the agenda and taking a good deal of the time. That time need not be wasted, however, if the tutor engages the writer dialogically. In the following excerpt from a tutorial session, the tutor (T) is working with a student to edit noun phrases. There is no direct correction; instead, the tutor guides the student to discover the error for herself.

Example 1

T: [reading the student's text] "We can see a grey big layers in the sky with a dense smog" What is...do you see anything wrong here?

S: Dense smog with ah heavy or...

T: That's fine, yeah this is good

S: This is good?

T: But what do you see wrong in these two sentences?

S: Ah just a moment. "We can...see we can...we can...see"

T: Uhum

S: It...grey

T: Okay

S: big

T: Okay, grey big

S: Layers

T: Layers

S: Layers in the sky

T: Uhum

S: Because is no one only, is all the...

T: Layers, it is not singular. Right, that's good

S: Grey big layers...yes (laughs)

T: In the sky

S: With...dense

T: Okay

S: (laughs)

T: Dense, that's good

S: Dense smoke

T: With dense smog

S: "Produced by carbon monoxide of the the vehicle"

(from Aljaafreh & Lantolf, 1994, p. 477)

The tutor here merely locates the grammatical errors (two unnecessary indefinite articles) and then prompts the student to find the structural inconsistency in the phrases *a grey big layers* and *a dense smog* on her own and to self-correct them. Along the way, the tutor provides positive feedback on other parts of her text.

Corrective feedback on grammar can also take place during peer tutoring. In the next excerpt two advanced ESL writers are working together to polish a text one of them (S2) has written. The other takes over the role of tutor and at one point focuses on a sentence of the text that reads: *And I was impressed how can a house could be so far from the road.*

Example 2

[1]   *S1:*   So...what is it that you want, you did it, you tell me what you were doing. You say here that you passed along some little houses made of wood and you were impressed...

[2]   *S2:*   ...at how those houses could be so far from the roads...

[3]   *S1:*   Then you are asking yourself...

[4]   *S2:*   Well, I was not asking but commenting...

[5]   *S1:*   Because if you use *how*, it's because you were asking something. *How* is used to make questions, do you understand?

[6]   *S2:*   Yes.

[7]	*S1:*	Because…look…tell me if it doesn't sound better. I want you to give me your opinion. You say that you passed along some houses made of wood and that you were impressed at how, see? If I say *"at how"*…in Spanish…a thing could be…a house could be…see? There's a redundancy.
[8]	*S2:*	Hmmm…
[9]	*S1:*	*"I was impressed at how can a house could be"* how can a house…
[10]	*S2:*	It would be then *"at how a house could be…"*
[11]	*S1:*	*"how can a house be…"*
[12]	*S2:*	again?
[13]	*S1:*	or *"how can a house…"*
[14]	*S2:*	No.
[15]	*S1:*	There's a very subtle detail here. *"I was impressed how, how can a house be…"* This doesn't sound right.
[16]	*S2:*	And, what about *"how a house could"* without *"can"*?
[17]	*S1:*	Exactly, I think it sounds better *"…how a house could be…"* so this *"can"* doesn't go there…

(from De Guerrero & Villamil, 2000, p. 60)

Here the peer as tutor (S1) has isolated the error but doesn't have a clear notion of how to fix it. Indeed, he is not exactly sure what the error is. Through the conversation it becomes clear to S1 that S2 does not intend the sentence to ask a question (passages 3–4), although S1 is not able to come up with the correct structure (passages 5–9). Finally S2 arrives at the solution, which is then confirmed by S1 (passages 16–17). By dialoging with each other and drawing on their implicit knowledge of English grammar (Williams, 2002), they finally hit upon a phrase that sounds right.

Clarifying Meaning

In addition to providing feedback on language errors, tutors also serve as sounding boards for L2 writers to test out the clarity of their expressions. In conversations like the one that follows, reported by Williams (2002), the tutor directs the L2 writer's attention to places in the text that are likely to be confusing for other readers (Williams' transcription conventions have been retained. Each [.] represents a half-second pause. O = tutor; L = student writer.)

Example 3

[1] *L:* This paragraph it's about ... he discover his father experience.

[2] *O:* mmhm . The discovery of his experience, right?

[3] *L:* His father life . in the past.

[4] *O:* He finds out the truth about his father's past?

[5] *L:* The truth about Japanese.

[6] *O:* About Japanese-Americans?

[7] *L:* uh huh .. being. It's about his father life.

[8] *O:* mmhm . His father's life.

[9] *L:* ..um .. (writes) . The father's life.

[10] *O:* mmhm . So what's next? .. So all of this is about that one sentence?

[11] *L:* mmhm.

[12] *O:* Kay. And this one is about?

[13] *L:* Relationship between . father. Of his father and himself.

[14] *O:* About his father and his father's father?

[15] *L:* uh huh. So, it's .. well . his father treated him like . his grandfather treated his father .. so it's like.relationship?

[16] *O:* mmhm. Mkay. So, his father had a similar relationship with his own father?

This tutor is serving as the writer's preliminary audience, providing her with feedback on portions of the text that do not clearly convey her intended meaning (passages 10–12). At the same time he provides her with bits of language that she can use to fill in the holes in her text (passages 4, 8, and 16).

Discovering Ideas

Tutorial talk is not limited to solving sentence-level problems. Muriel Harris (1990) illustrates how ideas for a student's text are generated, expanded, and refined though dialogue. In this example an L1 writer is talking with her tutor about a paragraph in her text that isn't going the way she wants it to.

Example 4

S: I think that paragraph about how I set up the tent—it needs something. But what? I'm...it's not strong. It...what I want to say about getting the tent up is it's so complicated.

T: Complicated. That's a good word to think about. Here, in this sentence you used the word "complicated," but I didn't know what you really meant. What's complicated about putting up a tent?

S: For one thing, my dad had to show me how to lay it flat on the ground. When you start—and you unfold the tent—you have to lay it really flat. And then the rain flaps go in a certain way. Then, the pegs need to be set so you—so the tent is tight when it goes up.

T: Oh, I didn't know that. How about putting those details in the paragraph? Here...right here, what about right after this sentence?...

(from Harris, 1990, pp. 149–150)

Harris (1995) refers to this kind of dialogue as "exploratory" talk, as opposed to the "presentational" talk that commonly occurs between teacher and students in the classroom (see the discussion of the IRE teaching script in Chapter 4). Exploratory talk is neither premeditated nor predetermined; it takes place only when the dialogic structure of the talk is flexible enough to allow students as well as tutors to initiate topics and play the role of informant. In Example 4, the tutor listens to the student writer explore her options and helps her to identify possible material to include in the text.

Arranging Ideas

Tutors also deal with issues of arrangement in their L2 student writers' texts. Organization problems can arise regardless of the student's proficiency level. In fact, for advanced L2 writers working on sophisticated assignments, organization may be the major issue in the early drafts. In the next excerpt a tutor talks with Najiba (N), an L2 doctoral student in the field of special education, about the organization of the literature review chapter of her dissertation, which deals with special education programs and L1-Arabic children in U.S. schools.

Example 5

[1] *T:* Okay, here's an inconsistency. See, "Assessment" as a main topic is only one page and a little bit more. About one page.

[2] *N:* Uh huh.

[3] *T:* That's not enough. I don't think that's enough for one major topic. So it doesn't look like it's a major topic. It looks like it should be part of something [else]... you know what I mean?

[4] *N:* OK.

[5] *T:* Your other major topics are 3, 4 pages long, you know?...until you get to this one. I mean this is big. This is the rest of the chapter...just about...but this one is only one page.

[6] *N:* Yeah. So it's either, you mean like it shouldn't be either a main topic or...

[7] *T:* It should not be a main topic

[8]   *N:*   It should be included or if I use it as a main topic, so I should, you know, add more.

[9]   *T:*   Right. The easy thing to do, I think, would be to include this in one of the other topics and take it out as a main topic.

[10]   *N:*   Um.

[11]   *T:*   Sub...you know,...subsume it under another, um, section. If you, if you did that, where would it most likely go? Would it, would it be better to put it here, under this topic or would it be better to put it under this topic?

[12]   *N:*   No it would be...Yeah...before talking about the IQ and creativity. Because IQ and creativity are assessments also, like assessment,...a way of assessing the kids.

[13]   *T:*   Okay.

(from Weissberg, 2006)

The issue here is the relative length of sections in Najiba's chapter. Her draft presents a problem of balance—one of the subsections is noticeably shorter than the other subsections. Although the draft contains many other minor problems, this excerpt is representative of much of the session, which is almost entirely devoted to issues of organization. Evidently the tutor has decided that these constitute a more critical problem than the sentence-level errors.

Learning Writing Strategies

Tutors may also take advantage of problems in their clients' drafts to address composition issues beyond the text immediately at hand. One issue likely to come up with novice L2 writers is that of general writing strategies. Expert writers have an active repertoire of techniques for planning, drafting, and improving their texts, and the writing tutorial is an ideal opportunity for them to pass them on to their clients (Harris, 1995; Sperling, 1991). Tutors may identify and recommend strategies that the student has not yet acquired (e.g., topic outlining). Or they may work with students to refine strategies they have already started to develop. In the next example, the tutor builds on his student's preexisting knowledge of cohesive devices to make a more global strategic point:

Example 6

[1] *T:*   You need to use a transition here, a joining word or phrase, something to help the reader make the connection between this paragraph and the next one…

[2] *S:*   …like using "therefore"?

[3] *T:*   Sure, that's a good connecting word. But can you see why readers need such words?

[4] *S:*   I suppose so. I know the book says we should use transitions. And there's that example paragraph in the chapter. But I think it makes my writing sound too formal… "Therefore" is like something you'd see in an encyclopedia.

[5] *T:*   Sure, I know what you mean. So what you're saying is that you need a list of words that are more natural for you…

(from Harris, 1990, p. 153)

Building on the student's preexisting knowledge is a critical feature of tutor talk, and one that fits well with the sociocultural view of tutoring as a form of assisted learning (Aljaafreh & Lantolf, 1994; Ohta, 2001). In Example 6, the tutor sees the need for a more cohesive text but also acknowledges his student's reluctance to use what she sees as a pretentious-sounding word. The one-to-one setting makes it possible for the tutor to identify and highlight a writing strategy that the student is underutilizing, while being careful to validate her sense of her own writing style.

The technique illustrated by the tutor in Example 6 offers us a critical insight into one of the hallmarks of good tutoring: directed, conversational dialogue used by tutors to create

scaffolded learning for their learners. This is the topic of the next section.

Scaffolding

Like instructional conversations in whole-class teaching, successful writing tutorials consist of a skillful blend of conversation and teaching. How do expert tutors embed their instruction in dialogue? The centerpiece technique is known as **scaffolding,** a dialogic process in which tutors identify appropriate tasks and then help their student writers to accomplish them through conversation (De Guerrero & Villamil, 2000; Donato, 1994; Williams, 2002). Jerome Bruner and his colleagues (Wood, Bruner, & Ross, 1976) first used the term *scaffolding* to describe the instructional assistance given to children by adult tutors—often their parents. They defined it as the "process that enables a child or novice to solve a problem, carry out a task or achieve a goal which would be beyond his unassisted efforts" (p. 90). The notion of scaffolding has more recently been applied to instructional conversations "in which a knowledgeable participant can create, by means of speech, supportive conditions in which the novice can participate in, and extend current skills and knowledge to higher levels of competence" (Donato, 1994, p. 40). In Vygotskian terms, scaffolding is the oral means by which tutors help their students to negotiate their way through the zone of proximal development (or ZPD—see an earlier discussion in Chapter 2).

For an example of scaffolding in the context of an L2 writing tutorial, let's look again at Example 5 on pages 85–86. The tutor first identifies the organizational problem (passages 1–5), then allows Najiba to come up with a solution (passages 6–8), which he subsequently confirms (passages 9–11). In the last three passages (11–13) he turns the final details of the solution back to Najiba. In effect, he creates a learning environment in which his client can, with help, find her own solution to a difficult composition problem.

Annemarie Palincsar (1986) clarifies the construction metaphor implicit in the word *scaffold* when she notes that, like the superstructure around a building under construction, an oral scaffold is a means of providing support for the student that is both "adjustable and temporary" (p. 75). That is, the tutor provides precisely the kind of support that a student writer needs at a given moment and then withdraws the support as soon as the writer appears able to function without it. How do tutors construct these adjustable, temporary superstructures? The next section describes four strategies that tutors use as they build oral scaffolds.

Get the Student Talking

In a writing conference, no scaffolding can take place without the active oral participation of the student writer. The tutor engineers the dialogue, but in order for it to be truly collaborative the student writer must be responsible for generating some of the discussion. How does one get such a conversation off the ground, especially with L2 writers who are naturally reticent or who may be used to playing a more passive role in instructional settings? One way is to structure the tutorial conversation *in advance* to ensure some student participation. Some tutors, for example, let their students know before their scheduled meeting that they are responsible for deciding what to talk about during the session—in other words, to bring a tentative agenda with them. If the student has anticipated the conference by preparing a topic or two for discussion, there is a better likelihood of developing scaffolded dialogues than if he or she simply shows up to see what the tutor will say about his or her paper.

Giving positive feedback about specific aspects of their writing is another way for tutors to stimulate a student to participate orally (e.g., *This section is really clear! How did you do it?*). The praise helps a timid student build the self-confidence necessary to play an active role in the conversation, while the follow-up question gives her a direction to follow. As with the student agenda technique just described, the objective of giving positive feedback is to ease the student into the role of proactive participant in the conversation.

Tutors also get their students talking by having them start off the session by reading their drafts aloud. As the student reads her draft, some of the more obvious problems will jump out at her, giving her the first chance to correct them (Brooks, 1991). Or the tutor can read the text aloud, with the student listening and stopping the tutor when she perceives a troublespot. In either case it's the student, not the tutor, who makes the actual changes/corrections on the paper; whoever reads aloud, the responsibility for critiquing the text falls first to the student, with the tutor providing backup help.

Maintain Conversational Parity

As Rebecca Jackson (2002) notes, one of the main goals of conferencing is "to move writers toward greater independence and self-sufficiency, to help them acquire the skills, processes and habits of mind of more experienced writers" (p. 375). The student's independence and self-sufficiency are more likely to be strengthened when tutor and student share the responsibility for building the conference dialogue. Thus, once the tutor has established that it's acceptable for the client to be an active participant in the session, successful scaffolding depends on roughly equal participation—tutor and student building a dialogue mutually, without either one consistently monopolizing the conversation.

Parity is to some degree a quantitative issue, the number and length of teacher and student talk-turns being roughly equivalent. Absolute parity in each segment of the dialogue is not necessary for scaffolding to occur; as in any conversation, there will be a tendency for one party to take charge of the discourse from time to time. However, the tutor must be sensitive to the parity issue to ensure that he or she is not hindering the student's participation. Achieving even rough parity in a tutorial conversation is not easy; as already noted, it is often difficult for teachers (or tutors with teaching experience) to shift gears and dialogue with, rather than lecture to, student writers.

Achieving parity in tutorial conversations also implies that a tutor be a good listener (Harris, 1990). By attending to the student throughout the tutorial, the tutor learns what the student writer already knows about the topic, the assignment, the text at hand, and about his or her general level of writing expertise. These constitute the student's knowledge base, the information and experiences he or she brings to the conference. When the tutor understands this, he or she is in a better position to establish appropriate tasks for the writer to accomplish within the ZPD. This is a far different strategy from a one-way transfer of information from tutor to student based on the tutor's knowledge base.

Recognizing the student's areas of expertise is another strategy tutors use to achieve parity. The lion's share of expertise in a writing conference is typically held by the tutor, whose experience and training in writing usually far exceed the student's. This asymmetry is often reflected in the disproportionate amount of talk-time taken by the tutor. To offset this, the tutor can see to it that the student writer holds the conversational floor when it comes to his or her area of expertise: the ideas and experiences that lie behind the written text. When the client's areas of expertise are acknowledged by the tutor and when he or she is given adequate time during the conference to talk about them, a more collaborative session is likely to result.

Ask Leading Questions

At transitional points in the session, a skillful tutor initiates new scaffolds by posing a leading question that nudges the student into an area she might not have investigated on her own (North, 1984, p. 78). Leading questions might deal with sentence-level problems (e.g., *What do you mean by this sentence?*), global discourse features (e.g., *Can you show me your thesis? What kind of problems did you have in organizing the main points?*), or revision (*Are there any places where you think the organization could be improved?*). Asking a leading question is more likely to promote scaffolded conversation than for the tutor to simply point out a problem area and advise the writer how to fix it.

Leading questions are also used by tutors as a framing technique to initiate or conclude a conference. The tutor may start out by asking the student to talk about the paper and the difficulties that were encountered in writing it (e.g., *How did this draft go for you? What problems did you run into while you were working on this draft?*), or he or she may begin by finding out what the student likes and dislikes about the draft. To signal the end of the conference, the tutor might ask the student to generalize and reflect on the draft in progress (e.g., *So, what do you think about the paper overall?*).

Link and Extend

Finally, it's helpful to look at a tutor's oral scaffolding meta-phorically, as essentially a process of **forging links** and **creating extensions.** From this perspective the tutor's task is two-fold: (1) to use uptake (see Chapter 4) to establish dialogic links to the client's side of the conversation, and then (2) to use those links as springboards to a teaching point. The metaphors of linking and extending fit well with the underlying metaphor of the physical scaffold—a temporary structure that attaches to a primary structure and that is used to build it up. There are at least two ways tutors do this.

Verbal Linkages

On the linguistic level, the tutor creates links by deliberately echoing bits of language from the student's side of the dialogue (single key words or longer phrases) in his or her rejoinders, as in the tutor's repetition of the student's word "complicated" in Example 4 (p. 84). In this way the tutor creates clear cohesive markers that link what the student has said to a new idea or an instructional point. Similar verbal linkages can be seen in Example 5, passages 6–9, where the tutor incorporates Najiba's noun *main topic,* her auxiliary *should,* and her verb *include* in his responses. By creating cohesive links through repetition, the tutor acknowledges the student's ideas as salient and that he respects her as a contributing partner in the dialogue. In doing so, his own comments are likely to achieve more relevance in the student's eyes.

Idea Linkages

Palinscar (1986) notes that effective tutors respond to *what* their student clients say, not just to how they say it. This means that the tutor works not only to connect with the client on the linguistic level, but also to incorporate the client's ideas into the scaffolded dialogue. The tutor may accomplish this by paraphrasing or summarizing the student's earlier contributions before going on to a teaching point. Again, by doing so the tutor acknowledges and legitimizes the student's contributions and uses them as springboards to a more sophisticated task or insight. Idea linkage can be seen in Example 6, passages 2 and 3, where the tutor acknowledges the student's example *therefore* (but does not repeat it verbatim), and in passages 4 and 5, where he paraphrases the student's feelings about formal register.

Idea linkage is a more sophisticated way of establishing connections than is direct repetition, but both accomplish the same thing—they allow the tutor to connect his oral scaffold to the student's side of the dialogue and then use it as a platform for further instruction.

Training Tutors in the Dialogic Model

As shown, an effective writing tutorial depends on the tutor's skill in building oral scaffolds for the client. This is not a simple task. As Lynn Goldstein and Susan Conrad (1990) point out in their article on ESL writing conferences, a high-quality tutorial dialogue doesn't happen simply by virtue of putting a tutor, a willing student, and the student's text together in the same room. Like any complex instructional task, conducting effective, interactive writing conferences takes training, experience, and some conscious reflection on the tutor's part.

These complexities are compounded by institutional forces that work against dialogic tutoring—the teacher-like discourse habits that many tutors unconsciously bring to their tutorial sessions (Wong, 1988), and the pervasive influence of the education hierarchy, which assigns students to a relatively powerless position in comparison to that of instructors, and encourages passive behavior in tutoring conversations. Both tutors and students can become accomplices in reinforcing each other's institutionalized roles, whether they intend to or not (Bawarshi & Pelkowski, 1999; Thonus, 1999b). Add to this the tight tutorial schedule that college writing centers must adopt to accommodate large numbers of students, and there may be little time for tutors and their clients to establish collaborative relationships.

Pre-Service Training

To counteract these influences, tutors can benefit from pre-services and in-service training in dialogic conferencing techniques (Bruffee, 1995; Grabill, 1994). In pre-service training, new tutors become acquainted with the techniques of oral scaffolding—how to encourage conversation when their clients don't know how or don't want to talk about their writing; how to keep the conversation going without co-opting it; how to keep the tutorial dialogue on task, yet relaxed and informal; and how to create linkages and extensions as they converse with their clients. Group discussions and role-plays are good ways to train tutors in these aspects of dialogic tutoring, with experienced tutors serving as peer trainers and consultants.

A reading packet consisting of published articles like those referenced in this chapter can be provided for new tutors to acquaint them with specific issues they will face when conferencing with L2 writers. They will learn, for example, that dealing with the language issues peculiar to L2 writers (e.g., problems in syntax, word choice, and expression) is only part of the game; they are also likely to encounter rhetorical problems in their clients' papers resulting from differences between the L2 learner's native language and written academic

English. Rhetorical aspects of academic English include specific techniques for focusing on a topic, the appropriate use of outside sources, ways of making and substantiating claims, the degree of personalization in a text, and methods of constructing arguments—these can be quite different from the rules and expectations of the student's L1 (Harris, 1986; Leki, 1992). Tutors who are aware of these issues will be better prepared to address them dialogically with their clients.

In-Service Training

Pre-service training should be followed by a supervised in-service practicum. Initially, it's important for new tutors to become aware of their own discourse styles and to realize how easy it is to fall into repetitive, teacher-like patterns of talk that undermine collaborative dialogue. Thus, an important part of in-service training is for tutors to conduct a **discourse audit** of their own conversational styles, similar to the audit discussed in Chapter 4 for classroom teachers. Tutors-in-training might record one of their own tutorial sessions, analyze it for discourse patterns, look for evidence of oral scaffolding, and identify points in the session where opportunities for scaffolding may have been missed. For example, some tutors may hear themselves making many directive statements to their students, rather than promoting exploratory talk through dialogically linked comments and questions. Or tutors may find that in their eagerness to make a teaching point, they virtually ignore their client's side of the dialogue, and thus effectively prevent scaffolding from taking place. The audit will highlight such tendencies, which is something tutors can address in later sessions with their clients or in subsequent training sessions.

At this point, new tutors should also be introduced to the critical issue of how power and authority are brokered in tutorial sessions with L2 writers. As previously mentioned, writers from some cultural backgrounds may be uncomfortable participating in a peer-like relationship with a tutor. Some international students, especially those coming from authoritarian educational systems, may be confused by, and even suspicious of, a tutor who doesn't play the expected role of an authority figure. In these situations, tutors may find that they need to adopt a more directive attitude with their L2 clients than they do with L1 writers, as some researchers have suggested (Blau & Hall, 2002; Powers, 1993; Thonus, 1999b; Williams, 2002). However, the point should be made during training that increased directiveness need not come at the expense of scaffolded instruction. Indeed, from a dialogic point of view, the tutor's principal job is to act as a coach—to set a sequence of tasks within the student writer's ZPD and to help her accomplish each one through structured dialogue (Ohta, 1995). Obviously tutors must exert a certain degree of control in their conversations with clients to accomplish this.

An important point to be made to new tutors during training is that each L2 client must be treated as an individual learner. No single, one-size-fits-all tutorial package will work for everyone (Patthey-Chavez & Ferris, 1997; Sperling, 1991). That being said, most of the issues that arise in tutoring L2 writers can be addressed through dialogue; in fact, each problem found in an L2 student's paper can be looked at as an opportunity for the tutor to engage in dialogic scaffolding with his client.

Is Scaffolded Instruction Worth the Effort?

As the new tutor soon learns, scaffolded instruction is labor-intensive. When a 5-minute teaching point turns into a 30-minute discussion with a client, the tutor must keep in mind that dialogic teaching is a long-term investment in an L2 student's writing development, one that leads to long-term changes in the writer's ability to make good linguistic and rhetorical choices (Goldstein & Conrad, 1990; Leki, 1992; Powers, 1993; Williams, 2004). Understanding these practical benefits will help the tutor find the patience to see extended and sometimes tiring sessions with their clients through to the end.

First, it will help tutors to know that the dialogic approach will help their L2 students to **analyze their professors' writing assignments rhetorically.** Through conversations with their tutors, students can learn to ask themselves questions like, *What does this instructor want? What am I expected to do? How does this assignment fit in with the rest of the course?* for each writing project they face. This ability to view a writing project in its wider rhetorical setting is a strategic skill that good academic writers use, and it's a particularly important one for students who are new to the academic community and who may be unsure of its expectations.

Second, tutors should be aware that by taking the time to dialogue with their L2 writers they are helping them to develop **a critical approach to reading academic texts,** including their own. This allows the writing tutorial to become a training ground where L2 students can learn to act like members of an academic community—selecting from, questioning, and "conversing" with other authors' works; agreeing with some and disagreeing with others; and marshalling their source writers' ideas to help them in making their own points. When tutors nudge their L2 clients into habits of critical reading, they help them to model what expert academic writers do when they read potential sources. They learn to ask themselves questions like, *Can I use this source? If so, how? Is this author offering anything new? Do I basically agree or disagree with what he/she says?*; and when reading their own texts, asking *Am I making the most effective argument I can in this paper?* Learning to ask questions like these leads L2 learners to habits of critical thinking that will help them achieve success in their academic disciplines. It's a skill that tutors can help their L2 writers internalize by prompting them orally with the same kinds of questions during their sessions.

Finally, it's important for overworked tutors to realize that by taking additional time to dialogue with their L2 students they are helping them to develop **a personal voice** in their writing. As Leki (1992) notes, L2 writers often find it difficult to "find their own voices" in written English (p. 68); indeed, there is some debate over the merits of even trying to help L2 writers in this area (Ramanathan & Atkinson, 1999). On the other hand, tutors who accept the basic premises of the dialogic approach to teaching writing will appreciate the critical role that a writer's oral voice plays in her literacy development. We will return to the controversial topic of voice in Chapter 7. For now, it's enough to say that the writing tutorial is an ideal setting for L2 writers to learn to trust their oral voices as a resource for writing.

Suggested Tasks and Discussion Questions

1. Find out how the **writing center** at your institution trains its tutors. What special training, if any, does it provide for tutors who work with L2 writers?

2. Compare the notion of **scaffolding** developed in this chapter with that of **instructional conversations** in Chapter 4. What areas of overlap do you see in these two strategies? How would you expect a teacher who practices the dialogue approach to alter his or her speaking style when moving from whole-class instruction to one-on-one tutoring?

3. **Observe and record a tutor colleague** working with an L2 writer in a session that lasts at least 30 minutes. Develop an observation protocol, and use it to analyze the one-to-one discourse you have recorded. Look for overall discourse patterns and evidence of scaffolding, if any, in the tutorial. Interview the tutor to get his or her perspectives on the session. Finally, assess the session from the point of view of dialogic teaching.

4. Use the evidence you collected in Task 3 to devise **a list of do's and don'ts** that you could distribute in a future training session for tutors of L2 writers.

Chapter 6
Written Response as Dialogue

*"Any remark on a student essay, whatever its form,
finally owes its meaning and impact to the governing
dialog that influences some student's reaction to it...the
larger conversation in which it plays a part."*
(Knoblauch & Brannon, 1981, p. 3)

The students in an intermediate ESL writing class at a community college have been assigned to write an essay about "a person you admire." One of the students, Mauricio, the son of migrant farmworkers, submits the following piece:

Lalo Huerta

Lalo Huerta is my father. He is married to my mother Elvira Huerta. They have 2 sons and 2 daughters. The first is me the second is my brother Daniel the third is my sister Ruby the last one is my baby sister Jennifer. I admire my dad because he raise us and he did a lot of things for this family and thanks to him we are here in the U.S. and here in college.

I admire my dad because he has accomplished a lot of things that he wanted to do. For example he decided to come to live to the U.S. but at first we couldn't because we did not have permission to come to the US. At first he tried to be resident of the US and work hard at it and finally he got it. But that did not satisfied him he wanted all his family to be residents like he is. So he investigated and he finally got us to be residents of US like he was.

The other thing that I admire of him is that he wanted a better life for his family. He encourages me to come to college. He wanted me to get a better job than the one that he had. So he told me that he wanted more education for us and he help me and support me and that is one of the reasons that I am in college now.

Those two reasons are why I admire him. Thanks to him I am here in the US. And that is why I am here in college. That is why I chose him as the person that I admire most in my life. I hope that when I grow up I will do the same thing for my family like he did for us.

Mauricio Huerta

Mauricio is a first-generation college student in a special admissions program and like many in the program, he is at risk of dropping out during his first year. Not wanting to discourage him by correcting all the mechanical errors in the paper, his instructor writes only the following comments as an endnote on the last page of the essay:

Example 1

- -

Mauricio, I can follow this really easily. It's clear and it gives me a good picture of your father. To fill out the "essay blueprint," I'm going to ask you to add a couple of things to this draft: First, add a <u>controlling idea</u> to the thesis statement. Second, give more <u>support</u> to ¶2 and 3. How about some specific information, like what kind of work your dad is doing? (As it is, the 3rd ¶ is too short to stand alone.) Can you do that? What else could you add to ¶2 to beef it up a little? (By the way, you'd better check your sentence punctuation. There are a lot of run-ons.)

The teacher's comments and Mauricio's subsequent responses constitute the first phase in **a written dialogue** that will continue throughout the semester, running parallel with in-class discourse, conference talk, and the formal writing assignments in the course. In setting up this parallel dialogue-in-writing with Mauricio, the teacher is attempting to carry over the conversational dynamics of her classroom into the written phase of her instruction.

In doing so she is following Dana Ferris's (2003) advice that "writing instructors need to think of written feedback as part of dynamic two-way communication between the teacher and the student" (p. 124). This chapter considers a number of ways in which teachers of L2 writers can create this kind of communication in their written commentary to their students by applying the dialogic model. Each section examines a different avenue available to writing instructors for engaging their students in written dialogue. As in the earlier chapters, special attention will be paid to the benefits and caveats that a dialogic model of written response implies for L2 writers.

Since writing comments on students' drafts is the most frequent kind of academic writing that many teachers do (Elbow, 2002), much of this chapter deals with these responses and how they can be made interactive. However, it also looks at several other written applications of the dialogue model in the writing classroom, including electronic communication, all of which teachers can use to continue and extend what Knoblauch and Brannon (1981) call "the larger conversation" of the writing classroom.

Written Comments as Conversation

Dialogue is built into the written responses teachers give their students about their writing whether they mean it to be or not (Gay, 1998). The typical response sequence in a writing class follows a three-step discourse pattern of (1) topic assignment ➜ (2) students' written response to the assignment ➜ (3) teacher's response to students' efforts. This pattern of writing and responding bears a strong resemblance to the IRE sequence of conversational moves that was noted as typical of the recitation script for classroom talk (see Chapter 4). Like the classroom discourse cycle, the writing/responding cycle can result in a non-productive, repetitive pattern, or it can be adapted to create dynamic written dialogues that actively support L2 students' writing development.

In order to use their comments to broaden and extend the dialogic quality of their instruction, teachers must become conscious of their written responses as part of the larger conversation they carry on with their student writers in and outside the physical classroom. To do that, instructors must analyze the salient features of their own written discourse just as they do their oral classroom teaching. The discourse features of written comments that must be attended to differ only slightly from those that affect oral communication between teacher and students in the classroom. First, the dialogic quality of written response depends on its degree of **personal involvement** (Tannen, 1985). How often we address students by name and how often we refer to ourselves affect the conversational quality of our written comments and reflect our level of personal investment in our students (Ferris, 2003). The **topic continuity** flowing through our comments is also important. When we write to a student about how a particular feature of his or her writing has changed over the course of a semester, or when we recall a comment made by the student in class or in an earlier assignment, we bring to our written comments the coherence of face-to-face conversation.

The dialogic quality of written comments also depends to some extent on **where on a student's paper** the comments appear. Teachers may mark incidental points throughout the student's text, either on the text itself or marginally; they may make general comments in the form of endnotes (as Mauricio's teacher did); or they may do both (see Ferris & Hedgcock, 2005, for a full discussion of this issue). Early studies on written response suggested that the placement of teachers' comments has no immediate effect on the quality of students' subsequent writing (see a review of this research in Knoblauch & Brannon, 1981). But the placement of comments does have dialogic consequences. Viewed as dialogue, personalized end comments are analogous to turn-taking in face-to-face conversation—one speaker listens and waits for a turn to talk, rather than interrupting the other speaker in mid-sentence.

A fourth factor affecting the dialogic quality of written comments is **the degree to which students participate** in the response process. Participation is partly determined by the number of opportunities students have to address the teacher's comments directly, in other words, to "talk back" (Lillis, 2003). Some techniques for making this option available to students will be examined later in the chapter. Another less obvious determiner of student participation is the degree to which the teacher's comments take into consideration **the student's own intentions in writing** the paper. As Knoblauch and Brannon (2002) point out, when judging and responding to their students' papers, teachers often do so by comparing them against an ideal template for the assignment that they carry in their own minds. Their written comments reflect this bias when they report back to students on how well (or how poorly) they succeeded in approximating the template and when they mandate changes in a student's text to make it conform more closely to the template (see Joy Reid's [1994] discussion of appropriating students' texts). This approach to response results in a monologue (Knoblauch & Brannon, 2002, p. 253) in which the teacher evaluates and reformulates students' writing but does not dialogue with them about it.

Other dialogic issues inherent in teachers' written comments include the **social stance** of the teacher versus student as projected through comments, and how teachers' individual comments can function as **speech acts** in a written conversation (Sperling & Freedman, 2001). The ways in which teachers manage these two factors, either to the enhancement or the detriment of dialogic instruction, is the subject of the next section.

Projecting a "Stance" through Written Comments

No comment written on a student's paper, whether it corrects a verb-tense error or critiques the strength of a student's argument, is socially neutral. On the contrary, writing teachers define themselves as social beings just as much through their written responses as through their oral interactions with their students in the classroom. Their attitudes, values, and relative social status as they perceive it in comparison to their students'—all are communicated through their written notes, comments, and corrections (Straub, 1999). Affecting all these forms of written communication are the teacher's underlying attitudes toward her students as writers, and in the case of L2 students, as language learners. The attitudes that she projects result in the creation of a **social stance** (i.e., a personal posture). For teachers of L2 writers, a useful discussion of stance is the one by Louise Phelps (1989), who proposes that writing teachers may take a continuum of social stances ranging from *evaluative* at one end to *socially and situationally contextualized* at the other, as evidenced by their written commentaries. Phelps claims that each point on this continuum marks a step in the progressive evolution of a teacher's philosophy toward her students as writers, toward the process of learning to write, and toward the role of written comments as a form of teacher-student communication (see Figure 8).

For the evaluative teacher, a student's text is a closed case—a complete, self-contained piece of writing that stands on its own. In her written comments, the teacher focuses on correcting errors and identifying those areas where the student's paper fails to match up with the assignment template that she has in mind. This stance is non-dialogic and may indicate that the teacher sees learning and instruction as a one-way process.

According to Phelps, as a writing teacher becomes more experienced, her attitude toward students' writing becomes more *formative;* that is, she tends to see a student's draft as one step in a sequence of drafts, each one an improvement

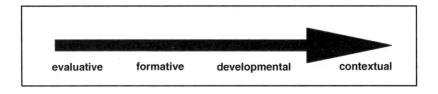

Figure 8. An evolving scale of teachers' attitudes as expressed in comments on students' written work (from Phelps, 1989).

over the last. This attitude is prevalent among teachers who subscribe to the process approach to teaching writing, who view composing as an individual, cognitive activity that develops through a series of fixed stages. These teachers' written comments may still focus on student errors, but they take the form of problem-solving advice, intended to help the student produce a better subsequent draft. The written comments of such a teacher likely contain more elements of dialogue than those of an evaluative teacher.

Still more evolved for Phelps are teachers whose approach to paper marking is *developmental.* They see a student's paper not just as one step in a sequence of drafts, but also as one indicator of a student's overall, long-term development and growth as a writer. These teachers' written comments tend to make note of improvements made or problems that persist over an extended series of written assignments.

At first glance the developmental stance would seem the most appropriate for teachers of L2 writers to assume. However, the most highly evolved posture for Phelps, and the one most consistent with the dialogic model, is taken by instructors who assume a *social context* stance when writing comments on their student papers. For a teacher at this stage, each new student paper is a literacy event in a long-running Bakhtinian dialogue—between student and teacher, among students working in groups, and in students' own minds as they struggle with the welter of contending voices and outside influences ("heteroglossia," in Bakhtin's terminology) that drive their composing processes and shape their texts (see Gay, 1998, for a discussion of written response from a Bakhtinian perspective). In the case of L2 writers, this conglomeration of contending voices may also include voices from their L1, especially for those who are experienced writers in their native language. The teacher's written comments add one more, albeit authoritative, voice to the internal dialogue being listened to and sorted out by the student writer.

The social context stance is appropriate from a dialogic as well as an L2 perspective. It encourages the teacher to see each student's paper not as an isolated attempt to imitate an expert written product, nor as a single stage in the student's development of L2 literacy, but as part of the larger conversation about writing that takes place both inside and outside the classroom. This is essentially the same social stance as that of the teacher who uses instructional conversations in her classroom teaching (see Chapter 4)—a verbally engaging, inclusive approach that encourages and respects students' contributions and weaves them into the ongoing instruction.

The writing instructor whose stance toward her students has developed to this point is probably well aware of the dialogic impact of her written comments, just as she is of the oral discourse taking place in her classroom. And it's no accident; as a practitioner of the dialogic approach she monitors the features of her individual written comments, just as she does her classroom speech, to gauge how well they work as dialogue. The next section examines some of the dialogic functions that written comments can play.

Written Comments as Speech Acts

To develop a sense of the dialogic functions of teachers' written comments, it's useful to view each comment as **a speech act** in an ongoing conversation. Dana Ferris and her colleagues (2003) conducted an extensive study of the comments written by one teacher on more than 100 ESL student essays. The investigators classified her comments into categories of speech acts based on their communicative purpose. They came up with the following categories:

1. Directives:
   - Asking for information, either already known to the teacher or not
   - Asking rhetorical questions
   - Making a suggestion or a request
   - Giving information, either text-based or reader-response type
2. Corrective comments about grammar & mechanics
3. Praise
4. Hedges (indirect politeness forms, e.g., "You <u>might consider</u> shortening the last sentence.")

(from Ferris et al., 1997, pp. 169-170)

Ferris and her colleagues went one step further and analyzed the linguistic form of the teacher's written comments as well. Just as in spoken language, they found that the teacher's comments fell into three syntactic categories: they were either statements, questions, or imperatives (one assumes there were truncated phrases as well as full sentences). While not condemning or praising any particular category of this teacher's written comments, Ferris and her colleagues point out that a teacher's written comments are unavoidably communicative, and as such they affect the relationship between the writer and the teacher, whatever the teacher's initial intentions in writing the comments may have been. Ferris et al. conclude that teachers interested in establishing and maintaining a dialogic relationship with their student writers must continually assess their own written comments as if they were moves in a conversation. The results of this assessment may lead them to make adjustments in the form, content, and the tone of the comments they write (Ferris et al., 1997).

A speech act analysis of the teacher's written responses that began this chapter (see Example 1 on page 100), and their communicative intentions, might yield the following results:

- -

1. Mauricio, I can follow this really easily. It's clear and it gives me a good picture of your father. **(Praise + confirmation – "I hear you and I understand you.")**
2. To fill out the "essay blueprint," I'm going to ask you to add a couple of things to this draft: First, add a <u>controlling idea</u> to the thesis statement. Second, give more support to ¶ 2 and 3. **(Suggestions–"These additions will make your paper even better.")**
3. How about some specific information, like what kind of work your dad is doing? **(Request for unknown information–"Tell me more.")**
4. As it is, the 3rd ¶ is too short to stand alone. **(Giving text-based critique–"This part doesn't work.")**
5. Can you do that? **(Polite request soliciting compliance)**

Mauricio's teacher is attempting to maintain a dialogic relationship with him through the conversational tone of her written comments. In contrast, a speech act analysis of another teacher's end comments on an L2 student's progress report demonstrates how failure to attend to written comments as speech acts can undermine the written dialogue:

Example 2

My Term Paper Progress

After five weeks of studies at this university, I learned many skills from English 25 course. One of the most important is writing term paper. I would like to write something about my term paper right now.

I scheduled my term paper writing progress into 10 parts....So far, I finished the first four steps and is proceeding to the 5th step. I hope I can speed up; otherwise it will be very busy on the end of November because it dues on December 4.

In order to type my term paper, I must learn how to operate Macintosh or PS/2 computers because I never use them before, especially two kinds of packages (Word 5.0 for Macintosh and WordPerfect for PS/2). As a result, I attended several lab classes offered by computer center. It is really interesting and I enjoyed it very much. It is useful for my future career too, and I think it is most challenging to me in writing my term paper.

(from Bates, Lane, & Lange, 1993)

- -

In this response, you have done a careful job of addressing both parts of the question and have illustrated your points with good specifics, including the names of word-processing programs. Good organization, too! **(Praise)** Because your organization is strong, I have marked most of your sentence-level errors as you requested. **(Reader response information)** I would suggest, however, that you first work on verb tense, verb form and articles. **(Corrective comment)** Also you will want to work on avoiding unclear references when you use the pronoun "it." **(Corrective comment)**

(from Bates et al., 1993, p. 78)

From the standpoint of dialogic instruction, these comments connect with little beyond the surface aspects of the student's paper; they project an aloof, non-dialogic stance on the teacher's part. Except for commenting on the student's use of a word-processing example, the instructor virtually ignores the content of the paper, a fact that is all the more striking since it is a highly personal reflection on the student's part. With the exception of the response to the student's earlier request for grammar correction, there is no attempt to draw the student into a dialogue about the paper or the work of producing it. Perhaps most interesting, from a discourse point of view, is the teacher's attempt to assign motive to the student *(Also you will want to work...)*, where in fact it is more probably an expression of the teacher's desire—an unusual speech act in a conversational context.

This example reveals that whatever a teacher's expertise in composition pedagogy may be, the crafting of dialogic written comments is a skill unto itself. As Robertson (1986) has noted:

> Before we draw on our years of academic training to tell a student how to revise, we need to rely on our common human experience to let a student know, 'I'm listening'... to respond to each [student] as we respond to a friend in conversation—with confirmation or dispute, an acknowledgment that we have heard and understood the message. (p. 90)

The next section offers specific suggestions for writing dialogue-based comments on students' papers.

Creating Written Dialogues with Students

Applying the dialogic model to their written comments requires teachers to couch their responses in conversational terms without sacrificing their persuasive authority as experts on writing. This is a crucial compromise since some L2 writers may be particularly sensitive to teachers whom they perceive as not projecting an authoritative image and therefore not to be taken seriously (Ferris & Hedgcock, 2005). Teacher comments expressed in a conversational yet authoritative voice sound like an extension of the dialogic teacher's classroom discussion style and will feel familiar and reassuring to such students, while at the same time inviting them to participate in a dialogue. One way to achieve this compromise is for the teacher to include features in her written comments that are borrowed from face-to-face conversation (Goldstein, 2004, 2005). The following suggestions will help teachers create this hybrid of writing and speech in their written comments.

Personalize the Feedback

As mentioned in Chapter 3, conversation (unlike most academic writing) is high in **personal involvement.** Dana Ferris (2003) recognizes the need to bridge this stylistic gap when she suggests that teachers address students by name when writing comments and that they sign their own names at the end. She also suggests that teachers include comments referring to progress (or lack thereof) in the student's writing from one assignment to the next, a signal of the teacher's personal attention to the student's development as a writer. Perhaps most important, she reminds us to "show interest in the student's ideas" (p. 119). This is no more than the etiquette one speaker extends to another when expressing interest and empathy in conversation.

Deal with Content First

Comments related to the **idea content** of a student's paper are by nature more dialogic than comments about the writer's form. From a dialogic perspective, feedback on grammatical or rhetorical form is somewhat like commenting on a person's pronunciation while he is trying to talk about a topic of concern. Obviously, L2 student writers do require, and often explicitly request, feedback on the formal accuracy of their writing, and most instructors do not wish to ignore the responsibility of providing corrective feedback. So this raises a dilemma: how to observe the dialogic ethic of focusing on L2 writers' ideas without neglecting their problems with formal accuracy.

One solution is to background the formal feedback—start off by dealing with the idea content of the student's paper and hold the corrective feedback until the end (Bates et al., 1993; Robertson, 1986; see also Example 1 on page 100). An initial comment like *Please check all your verbs for the correct tense* works well as a critique of a student's grammatical control, but is inappropriate dialogically. On the other hand, reserving formal feedback to the end of the comment (e.g., *By the way, you have a lot of verb tense errors in this paper. Can you clean them up before you turn in a second draft?*) identifies the same problem area but does so in a more conversational way.

Another option is to suspend all corrective feedback on mechanical errors for some assignments. Although the research evidence is fairly conclusive that L2 writers benefit from grammatical correction, this shouldn't be taken to mean that students necessarily benefit from repetitive, unrelenting nagging (Ferris & Hedgcock, 2005). Thus, to create a dialogic climate in their responses, teachers may set aside certain writing assignments, or particular drafts of one assignment, for content-only feedback.

Ask Questions

Comments couched as **questions** are more likely to create a sense of dialogue than are a series of statements (as in the teacher's comments in Example 2 on p. 109). As mentioned in the discussion of tutorial scaffolding (see Chapter 5), questions are used for a variety of pedagogic purposes, and this is no less true when applied to written comments. They can be addressed to the content of a student's paper (e.g., *This is interesting; where did you find this information?*) or to organization (e.g., *Why did you put this example here? Wouldn't it be better at the end?*). As in tutoring, teachers can use leading questions in their written comments to extend the student's thinking beyond the draft at hand (e.g., *How would you connect your conclusion to the introduction in your next draft?*). And questions need not be merely rhetorical; students can be given the opportunity to address their teacher's comments with responses of their own, as will be discussed in the final section of this chapter.

Just because a comment is phrased as a question, however, doesn't mean it necessarily functions as one in discourse or that it promotes dialogue (Knoblauch & Brannon, 2002). As in speech, written questions sometimes function as indirect speech acts; they may be statements, or even imperatives, in disguise. For example, *Is this a sentence?* written in the margin of a student's paper has the illocutionary force of an imperative (*Fix this fragment*). For a more dialogic response, an authentic question could be used instead; for example, *Is this a sentence?* could be rephrased as, *Do you see the punctuation problem here?*

As this example suggests, the use of questions makes the task of giving students written feedback more time consuming for the instructor than traditional paper marking. On the other hand, by taking advantage of the discourse power of authentic questions and other speech-like elements, the teacher can incorporate her written responses into the dialogue of the "larger conversation" of the writing class.

Help to Shape Not Appropriate

Just as it's poor etiquette to co-opt another speaker's side of the conversation for one's own purposes, it's bad dialogue manners for the instructor to use her written comments to try to force a student's paper to conform to an ideal text that the instructor already has in mind. This practice of taking over a student's writing is known as "appropriation" (Ferris, 2003; Ferris & Hedgcock, 2005; Knoblauch & Brannon, 2002). To maintain a dialogic approach in her written comments, the teacher avoids appropriating the student's paper by constraining her own responses to the student's intentions as evidenced in the paper. Her goal is to help the student realize those intentions as effectively as possible, not to re-do the text to fit a preconceived template. This may take more time and care on the teacher's part than reshaping the text, but it preserves the integrity of the student's purposes in writing the text.

This is not to say that instructors shouldn't alert students when their texts do not address an assignment adequately or when their texts are inappropriate (see Reid's [1994] discussion of the appropriation issue). What it does mean is that writing teachers avoid putting their own words or thoughts into their students' work or telling them what to think about the topics they write about. Goldstein (2004, 2005) points out that a viable alternative to appropriation is **intervention**—providing reliable corrective feedback while respecting students' rhetorical purposes:

> Commentary that ignores what a student's purpose is for a particular text and attempts either purposefully or accidentally to shift this purpose is appropriation; commentary that shows a student where he or she is not achieving her/his purpose(s) is helpful intervention;…commentary that "corrects" sentences or passages without asking the student about the intended meaning risks changing that meaning and thus risks appropriation; commentary that asks students what they want to say and then helps students find the language to do so is helpful intervention. (Goldstein, 2004, p. 68)

Avoid Hedging

As noted at the beginning of this section, for a writing teacher the art of writing dialogic comments is a compromise between sounding conversational and maintaining authority. One danger of incorporating politeness strategies from speech is that the teacher's intention may be blurred. Excessive politeness, hedges, or other indirect speech acts can be misunderstood by L2 writers and written off as incidental comments, not suggestions to be taken seriously (Ferris, 2003; Goldstein, 2005; Rafoth, 2004). Indirect speech acts that might be interpreted accurately by an L2 writer in face-to-face conversation (when accompanied by paralinguistic and non-verbal cues) may seem less straightforward when written out. To prevent misunderstandings, written comments to L2 writers should avoid excessive politeness. A hedged comment like, *I wonder if you've had a chance to look at the punctuation in this essay* could be passed off by the student as an idle question; it might be more effective restated as a direct request: *I noticed two fragments and three run-ons in your essay. Would you go back and fix those please?*

Let Students Talk Back

Dialogue can't take place if one of the interlocutors doesn't have an opportunity to respond. When students can't respond to their teacher's comments except through the revisions and corrections they make (or fail to make) in their subsequent drafts, the conversation is one-sided and in a sense is really no conversation at all. Students need a chance to respond to their teacher's comments in some form, to "talk back," so to speak, before committing themselves to another draft. There are a number of ways to build students' talk-back responses to teacher comments into the assignment cycle, which will be addressed later in this chapter.

Find Alternative Ways to Comment

To enhance the dialogic quality of their comments, teachers may make audio recordings of them for students rather than writing them (Anson, 1999). Comments can also be sent electronically; this is especially appropriate in situations where students are submitting their work electronically as well. (A fuller discussion of electronic communication follows.) Finally, a number of authors have suggested that teachers use their written commentaries to help set the agenda for face-to-face conferencing with the student writer (Brannon & Knoblauch, 1982; Ferris & Hedgcock, 2005; Goldstein, 2004). In this way, the teacher's written comments are absorbed into the "larger conversation" that begins in the classroom, continues on paper, and subsequently moves into the conference room.

Design Sequential Writing Assignments

We noted in Chapter 4 that using a content-based writing curriculum supports the teacher's efforts to bring dialogue into classroom instruction. In a similar way, a sequence of logically arranged and related writing assignments makes it easier for the instructor to provide her students with dialogic written feedback. As Ilona Leki (1990) has pointed out, when assignments in a writing course grow out of one another sequentially, it is easier for teachers to link their comments on one assignment to those they made on earlier assignments dealing with the same or similar issues. This helps them create a coherent on-paper conversation with each student writer that can last throughout an entire course.

Take, for example, an intermediate-level academic writing course designed to introduce L2 students to the process of writing a source-based paper. A series of assignments takes students from the early stage of selecting a topic to the last step of proofreading the final draft (see Menasche, 1997, for an example of such a task sequence). One of the assignments asks students to create a bibliography of tentative library sources for their papers. The teacher's written comment to one student on this assignment might refer back to an earlier one of narrowing the topic for the paper: *I can't figure out how these sources are going to help you with the topic you wrote about before. Have you changed your topic since the last assignment?* In general, the more inventive, interesting, and coherent the sequence of writing tasks is, the more it will facilitate the kind of written feedback that complements the dialogic approach.

At its worst, the task of writing comments on students' papers can produce some of the most formulaic language that teachers produce (Elbow, 2002). This is understandable; paper marking is often viewed as a tedious though necessary evil. Faced with a large stack of papers that must be handed back at the next class, a teacher will often dispense with the task as quickly as possible—marking the most serious of the errors in students' texts, adding a note of encouragement or warning at the end, and affixing a grade.

However, for teachers who consciously build dialogue into their instruction, writing responses to students, although time consuming, is a vital opportunity to engage them in written conversations about writing. With conscious attention to the speech acts they make on paper, they can break away from old habits of writing monologic comments. The choice is the teacher's; as Richard Straub (1999) reminds us:

> When all is said and done, our response styles are not determined by our personality. They are not determined by our institutional setting...And they are not set in stone. We create our styles by the choices we make on the page, in the ways we present our comments. (p. 149)

Other Conversations on Paper

In addition to writing comments, there are other ways in which teachers can dialogue with students on paper about their writing. This section examines a few that have been mentioned by L1 and L2 writing experts.

Comments-to-Comments

As previously mentioned, written response cannot be truly dialogic unless student writers have an opportunity to engage in the conversation. A number of techniques have been suggested for accomplishing this (Berzsenyi, 2001; Elbow, 2002; Ferris & Hedgcock, 2005; Gay, 1998; Goldstein, 2004). In Gay's version, students submit a cover sheet with their second drafts, indicating how they used (or didn't use) their instructor's comments to the first draft (see also Ferris & Hedgcock, 2005, for a similar technique). The comments-to-comments technique described by Berzsenyi consists of a stand-alone paper that students send back to their instructor, in which they write comments and ask questions provoked by the teacher's written responses to their first drafts. Joy Reid (1994) asks students to write "metacognitive memos" (p. 287) to inform the teacher about their "intentions, struggles and rationales" for a given writing assignment.

In another variation on **comments-to-comments,** Ilona Leki (1990) suggests providing students with a questionnaire for each written assignment they turn in, in which they evaluate the assignment and indicate what aspects of it they found particularly easy or difficult. Since some L2 writers feel uncomfortable responding directly to the instructor about her or his comments, Leki's questionnaire is a good alternative, since it formalizes the student-teacher correspondence with a set of pre-determined topics for students to respond to.

Whatever form they take, comments-to-comments serve some important dialogic functions: First, they give students the chance to answer back; they may use the opportunity to agree or disagree with the teacher's suggestions, to negotiate a different solution, or merely to ask for clarification. Second, the teacher can use students' comments to her comments to set the agenda for a subsequent student-teacher conference or tutorial. Perhaps most important, being given the opportunity to talk back signals to students that the last word on their written products is ultimately their own—that they must learn to trust their own judgments about the kinds of changes that are needed to improve their drafts.

Journals and Dialogue Papers

Patricia Stock at the University of Michigan developed a composition course expressly intended to integrate students' speaking and writing, using the former to inform and strengthen the latter. Her innovative course (described in Stock & Robinson, 1990) serves in many ways as an exemplar of the dialogic model of writing instruction discussed in this book. One of the most interesting features of her course is the variety of opportunities Stock gives her students to converse in writing, with herself and with each other, about their course papers.

In her syllabus she gives her students a preview of these activities:

> In this course we will study some of the uses of spoken and written language...we will use talk and writing as our means of learning about the powers and limitations of spoken and written language...What I am going to ask each of you to do is to identify a subject you know something about and that you

are trying to learn more about. Then, I'm going to ask you to talk about that subject both with members of this class and with me and then to write about the subject (1) for yourself in a *journal*—a place to "think on paper"; (2) for members of this class and me in *dialogue papers*—informal written conversations; and (3) for members of this class and me in *essays*. (Stock & Robinson, 1990, p. 167)

Stock's syllabus offers two suggestions for getting her students involved in written conversations about their writing. The **journal** is intended for the individual student's eyes only, while the **dialogue papers** (or "conversation papers") are shared with other members of each student's peer group. Both ask students to produce the kind of hybridized speech-as-writing previously discussed. The dialogue papers are especially interesting since they blend conventional brainstorming with written correspondence. In these papers, students address their ideas for their eventual essays to a specific audience—a group of fellow classmates—who have the opportunity to answer back in their small-group sessions or in their own dialogue papers.

Stock's other example of hybrid writing, the journal, is already familiar to many L2 instructors. A more dialogic version is the **dialogue journal,** which is passed back and forth between teacher and student and which many instructors use to get to know their students and to give them expressive writing practice (Peyton & Reed, 1990; Weissberg, 1998). In a writing course, the dialogue journal can be specifically devoted to discussing aspects of the student's writing. In this case the benefits of journal writing are focused and enhanced; not only does it open up a personal channel of communication between student and teacher, it also helps the teacher to raise students' awareness of the processes and problems they face in writing their formal assignments.

Similarly, Reid (1994), Rabkin and Smith (1990), and Chris Anson (2003) suggest keeping a **writing log** in which students record their class notes, thoughts about their writing assignments, pre-writings, and questions or comments for the teacher about their writing. The log is handed in periodically, and the teacher responds to it, in writing, as the situation demands.

Then the log is returned to the student, and the written conversation continues.

A potential problem for L2 writers with these response activities is the time and energy it takes to do them. Getting the primary essay assignment written may be difficult enough; the journals and dialogue papers can have the effect of turning one writing assignment into two or more. For this reason, teachers of L2 writers must keep in mind their students' capacities (and their own workload) when they assign the additional work of responding to comments. With these caveats in mind, the options discussed here for getting students involved in response are worth considering. They represent effective ways of breaking up the IRE-like cycle of "student writes/teacher comments/student re-writes" by introducing dialogic give-and-take between student and teacher, involving them both in written conversations about writing.

E-Conversations

Another way for instructors and students to dialogue about writing, in writing, is through computer technology. There is a good deal of evidence for the dialogic benefits of computer-mediated communication (CMC) in teaching writing. A number of university courses (composition as well as discipline based) have been designed to integrate CMC at regular intervals into their writing assignments (Coffin & Hewings, 2005; Doerfler & Davis, 1998; Kemp, 1998; Williams, 2005). Brookfield and Preskill (1999) show how the oral give-and-take of the real writing classroom can be simulated electronically in virtual classes—in distance learning and other Internet-based courses. Bloch (2002) shows how students and their writing instructors used CMC to accomplish a wide variety of communication functions, many of which students might not risk in face-to-face classroom interaction. Studies by Diane Belcher (1999) and Jeff Galin and Joan Latchaw (1998) reveal how CMC can level the discourse playing field and encourage L2 students, who might otherwise remain silent, to participate in the dialogue of a graduate seminar.

CMC can also be used to supplement conventional writing courses through the use of online writing labs, electronic mailing lists, chat rooms, electronic message boards, and e-conferencing. The last three will be discussed here.

Chat Rooms

The synchronous (real-time) interaction that occurs in computer chat rooms is the closest electronic equivalent to a classroom conversation. In fact, as Berzsenyi (2000) points out, it may be even better than the classroom version in at least one respect—chat tends to be more egalitarian than classroom oral discourse since reticent students may be more willing to participate in online discussions than they are in the classroom. Chat can serve as a safe substitute for face-to-face conversation for insecure L2 (as well as L1) speakers (Kemp, 1998; Yuan, 2003). Chat may also be more conversation-like than e-mail or other kinds of electronic talk because individual chat exchanges tend to be short and rapid (Berzsenyi, 2000), more like oral exchanges than written correspondence. Berzsenyi (2000) suggests that the teacher can help to level the playing field for all participants by actively coordinating, negotiating, and moderating chat-room conversations:

> As moderator, the teacher needs to make the best use of chat conferencing, allowing...students to develop strands of dialogue. Confused and inquisitive students also need the discursive space to articulate questions for clarification and elaboration. Like people in conversations, those in chat exchanges need some time to develop rapport, gather information and make decisions. (p. 168)

For some L2 students the advantages of the chat room may be offset by difficulties with language and/or unfamiliarity with computer technology. For example, one can predict problems for some L2 students due to insufficient keyboarding skills. Slower reading speech and response time may also limit the usefulness of chat for some learners. There is no doubt a steeper learning curve in chat for some L2 learners than for others, but that is not sufficient reason to avoid its use; after all, L1 writers also differ in their abilities to read, respond, and type. Chat can also be viewed developmentally, as an opportunity for L2 writers to hone their computer skills and perhaps even their oral language (Beauvois & Eledge, 1996, as cited in Belcher, 1999).

Instructors can use the chat room to discuss upcoming assignments, to help students in planning and developing written topics, and to provide feedback and discussion on completed assignments. And during chat sessions they can provide the same regulatory discourse functions that they do in their physical classrooms—raising and changing topics, allocating turns, and responding to and expanding students' contributions (Berzsenyi, 2000; Brookfield & Preskill, 1999).

Electronic Message Boards

Class message boards (also called electronic bulletin boards, discussion boards, class blogs, etc.) can provide a more teacher-centered approach to electronic conversations about writing. In the protocol used in one such course, the teacher established a topic on the e-board for discussion (e.g., *What's the best way to get sources for next week's essay homework assignment? What text differences can be found between a curriculum vita and a biographical statement?*). Students worked in teams to craft a response and then posted their group's comments on the board. Teams could then respond to posted comments by the other groups as well as directly to the teacher. The teacher could either interject occasionally or hold off commenting until all groups had weighed in. Finally, the teacher would sum up the discussion, critique the groups' responses, and announce a new topic or question (Robert Heiser, personal communication, 2005).

Unlike chat, the message board is an asynchronous (delayed, not real-time) form of CMC; however, it too opens the possibility for conversation-like negotiating within student groups and between groups and their instructor in the form of clarification requests, comprehension checks, and requests for confirmation (Williams, 2002). There is some evidence, in fact, that asynchronous CMC has some dialogic advantages over real-time chat in the quality of the dialogue produced, due precisely to the fact that its participants do not face the stress of either face-to-face or real-time electronic exchanges and can compose their comments and responses in a more relaxed setting (Belcher, 1999; Galin & Latchaw, 1998).

E-Conferencing

E-conferencing is an electronic version of the "comments-to-comments" technique described earlier. In distance learning courses it may take the place of teacher-student writing conferences as well. In e-conferences, students submit their written assignments to the instructor electronically, accompanied either by an e-mail cover letter attachment or by interpolating their own comments into the text of the assignment by using the "comments" function of their word-processing program, such as the one included in Microsoft Word (Goldstein, 2004). The teacher responds to the assignment via e-mail or by using a special computer application such as an electronic whiteboard (as described in a study by Hewett, forthcoming). The e-conferencing may continue through several iterations, with questions, comments, and responses passing back and forth until the student sends in a final draft.

E-conversations give L2 writers and their instructors another means of extending their dialogues about writing beyond the physical classroom. The technology involved may be initially unfamiliar and intimidating for some L2 writers (although certainly not for all, as Belcher, 1999, points out). However, after an initial shakedown period, CMC can help students become more involved in the work of the class and in their own writing assignments. As an added benefit, CMC gives L2 writers experience in computer skills that will serve them well later. And in distance learning and other online courses there may simply be no other means available for L2 writers to dialogue with their instructors and other classmates.

Written Response and the Larger Conversation

Viewed in the context of the dialogic approach, the teacher's written comments are not a departure from instructional conversations about writing; they are an integral part of it. As Knoblauch and Brannon (1981) established early on, written response is part of a larger conversation, a cycle of instructional dialogue that begins in the writing classroom, continues through successive drafts of students' papers, culminates in writing conferences and tutorials, and then resumes in the classroom (see Figure 9). Since it is impossible to separate teachers' written commentary from this larger conversation, the writing instructor's best option is to work toward realizing the full dialogic potential of her comments. To accomplish that, the social roles assumed by the instructor in writing comments, the stance and attitude expressed in the comments, and the discourse functions of specific written speech acts must be

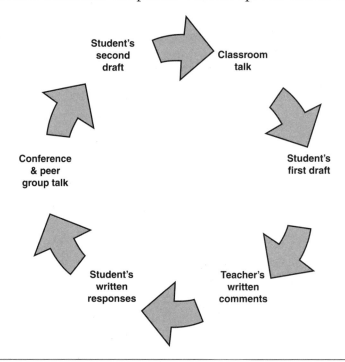

Figure 9. Written response and the "larger conversation" of writing class

taken into account since they all play a role in enhancing or reducing the dialogic value of the comments.

It is unlikely that Knoblauch and Brannon had L2 writers specifically in mind in their 1981 article, yet the critical role they claim for written response is as applicable for L2 as it is for L1 writers, if not more so. For L2 learners who use writing as a tool for their acquisition of the new language (Harklau, 2002; Reichelt, 1999; Weissberg, 1998, 2000), written conversations with their teachers are not just about learning to write, they are about learning language as well. For these writers, a teacher's written comments function as language input, the linguistic data that make it possible for them to acquire the sounds, structures, words, and social conventions of the new language. It seems reasonable that the more dialogic the instructor's comments are, the more salient they will be for the L2 learner and the better they will function as language input. Thus, for all writing teachers, but most especially for teachers of L2 writers, the dialogic potential of written response should not be ignored.

Suggested Tasks and Discussion Questions

1. Design a new writing course at the high school or college level with a strong **electronic component** built in. Show how the electronic component serves both the writing needs of the students and makes the course as a whole more dialogic.

2. Collect **samples of teachers' written responses** to student writing from various teachers you know who have L2 writers in their classes. Based on the samples, determine the approach to paper marking of each teacher based on Phelp's (1989) scale of teacher attitudes (see Figure 8 on page 105). Do the teachers in your sample seem to treat L1 and L2 writers differently in their written comments?

3. Select one of the more lengthy teacher comments from the sample you collected in Task 2. (Ideally, the comments you select should be directed toward an L2 writer.) Analyze each sentence in the sample, and determine the **speech act(s)** that it represents. Do any of the sentences represent **indirect speech acts** that an L2 writer might misinterpret? How would you assess the **dialogic value** of this teacher's written comments as a whole?

4. What is **your own approach to marking student papers?** How did you develop it? Does it involve any elements of teacher-student dialogue? As a writing teacher, what is your general reaction to the idea of "written response as dialogue" advanced in this chapter?

Chapter 7
Critiquing the Dialogue Approach

"[T]he road to dialog is rocky and full of pitfalls. But it beckons me as no other ever has."
(Sondra Perl, 2005a, p. xv)

In the previous six chapters we have, to paraphrase Sondra Perl (2005), taken the dialogue road in examining several aspects of teaching L2 writers: theoretical explanations for L2 literacy, individual differences among L2 speakers and writers, instructional conversations in writing classrooms, scaffolded learning in writing tutorials, and written conversations that take place between teachers and students outside the classroom. In each case a deliberate conversational emphasis in teaching and learning has been shown to open new insights and offer new possibilities for writing instructors and their L2 writers.

Throughout these discussions, the primary contention has been that dialogue-based writing instruction is especially beneficial for non-native writers. This claim is unlikely to meet with universal agreement among L2 writing practitioners; there are, in fact, some legitimate concerns with the dialogue approach, especially where L2 writers are involved. This last chapter steps back to take a broader more critical look at the dialogue approach. In the spirit of dialogue, the chapter poses, and then attempts to respond to, a series of questions about the efficacy of this approach and its appropriateness for L2 writers. The questions to be addressed will deal with issues concerning alternative interpretations of the term *dialogue,* an L2 view of the writer's *voice,* the controversy surrounding the usefulness of *peer writing groups,* and the *personal responsibilities* inherent in taking the dialogic approach.

Dialogue or Dialectic?

Is the dialogue approach no more than an updated version of the Socratic method? There is certainly nothing new about using conversational techniques in teaching. Twenty-five hundred years ago, Socrates demonstrated the art of dialogic teaching by engaging in question-and-response routines with his fellow Athenians (Hamilton, 1973; Rabkin & Smith, 1990), using logical reasoning. Socrates' method is a particular form of dialogue called **dialectic,** which consists of a linear sequence of questions by the tutor that serves to point out logical fallacies in his or her students' thinking and to help them arrive at truth through a process of logical induction. A famous example of Socratic dialogue shows the master leading his student, Phaedrus, to understand the superiority of speech over writing:

[1]   *Socrates:*   ...it shows great folly—as well as ignorance—to suppose that one can transmit or acquire clear and certain knowledge of an art through the medium of writing, or that written words can do more than remind the reader of what he already knows on any given subject.

[2]   *Phaedrus:*   Quite right.

[3]   *S:*   The fact is, Phaedrus, that writing involves a similar disadvantage to painting. The productions of painting look like living beings, but if you ask them a question they maintain a solemn silence. The same holds true of written words; you might suppose that they understand what they are saying, but if you ask them what they mean by anything they simply return the same answer over and over again...

[4]   *P:*   All that you say is absolutely true.

[5]   *S:*   Now can we distinguish another kind of communication which is the legitimate brother of written speech, and see how it comes into being and how much better and more effective it is?

[6]   *P:*   What kind do you mean and how does it come about?

[7]   *S:*   I mean the kind that is written on the soul of the hearer together with understanding; that knows how to defend itself, and can distinguish between those it should address and those in whose presence it should be silent.

[8]   *P:*   You mean the living and animate speech of a man with knowledge, of which written speech might fairly be called a kind of shadow.

[9]   *S:*   Exactly. Now tell me this. Would a sensible farmer take seed which he valued and wished to produce a crop and sow it in sober earnest in gardens of Adonis at midsummer, and take pleasure in seeing it reach its full perfection in eight days?...But where he is serious he will follow the true principles of agriculture and sow his seed in soil that suits it, and be well satisfied if what he has sown comes to maturity eight months later.

[10]   *P:*   You do well to distinguish, Socrates, between the farmer's serious business and what he might do in a different spirit.

[11]   *S:*   And are we to say that the man with real knowledge of right and beauty and good will treat what we may by analogy call his seed less intelligently than the farmer?

[12]   *P:*   Of course not.

[13]   *S:*   Then when he is in earnest he will not take a pen and sow his seed in the black fluid called ink, to produce discourses which cannot defend themselves *viva voce* or give any adequate account of the truth.

[14]   *P:*   Presumably not.

(from Hamilton, 1973, pp. 97–99)

Socrates' exchange with Phaedrus raises important questions about the nature of instructional conversations (see Chapter 4): *To what degree should instructional dialogues be focused and directed by the teacher? Who should hold ultimate power in determining where the dialogue goes and how it will end?* In dialectic, only one point of view, always the teacher's, prevails. Since the teacher's follow-up questions often negate the student's earlier responses, dialectic implies "tension, struggle [and] difference" (Lillis, 2003, p. 199). Socrates' dialectic is in fact much like the IRE pedagogy sequence discussed in Chapter 5—the teacher poses a question, the student responds, and the teacher evaluates the response and then continues by posing a new question. The teacher is thus the final arbiter over which (and whose) premises are acceptable and which are not. The resulting interaction in fact resembles more a courtroom cross-examination than an instructional conversation.

In contrast, the term *dialogue* as used throughout this book implies a joint, cooperative effort between teacher and student. Dialogue assumes a more egalitarian stance on the part of the teacher than does dialectic, and it offers a richer repertoire of discourse moves for both teacher and student. This is not to say that the dialogue approach negates the teacher's role as an instructional leader—indeed, the teacher plays an active and crucial leadership role—but it underlines the point that in building dialogues for learning, the teacher does not play cat-and-mouse dialectical games with his or her students; he or she uses dialogue as a naturalistic, social alternative to transmission-style teaching.

Some elements of Socratic dialogue overlap with the dialogic approach. Socrates depended on two-way, give-and-take to get his point across. He made extensive use of questions to draw his student into the conversation, and he did not dismiss his student's contributions out of hand. Indeed, he carefully wove Phaedrus's responses into his own line of argument (see passages 8 and 9 on page 129), a technique reminiscent of uptake (Chapter 4) and linking (Chapter 5). Most important, he seemed concerned for his student's welfare; although his immediate objective was to win the argument at hand, his ultimate goal was to bring his student along with him on a "pilgrimage best undertaken...by two like-minded people in collaboration and culminating in a mystical vision of reality" (Hamilton, 1973, p. 17).

Socrates' formal discourses certainly cannot be considered naturalistic conversational dialogue. He knew from the outset what the point of his lesson was and how he was going to get his tutee to arrive there. Each step in his sequence of questions was carefully calculated to move the student one step closer to his instructional goal, the discovery of truth (Hamilton, 1973). And we wouldn't go so far as to claim that his search for "a mystical vision of reality" is synonymous with the dialogic approach to teaching L2 writers as we have been developing it. Yet successful instructional conversations do contain a strong element of guidance and direction from the teacher. In that respect, they are no closer to naturalistic conversation than are Socrates' interrogations. Nor should they be; indeed, as shown in Chapter 5, L2 writers often appreciate the firm direction of tutors who behave as leaders rather than as peers (Thonus, 1999b; Williams, 2002).

In working with L2 writers, the goal then is to strike a balance between natural dialogue and dialectic. Perhaps the solution is for the writing instructor to be more willing than Socrates was to relinquish the reins of control from time to time. As we have seen, in writing tutorial situations and even in whole-class interaction, the dialogic teacher is prepared to cede temporary control over the direction of the conversation to students when that tactic appears to lead to a greater understanding of a writing issue. Socrates used dialogue to push his own agenda; dialogic writing teachers also have instructional agendas, but they are willing to entertain a number of ways to get there. Sometimes that means following the students' lead.

Dialogue, Bootstrapping, and Voice

As shown in earlier chapters, the dialogic approach has enjoyed a long tradition in the literature on L1 writing peda- gogy. As Peter Elbow, one of its foremost proponents, wrote two decades ago, "To exploit the speech-like qualities of writing as we teach is a way of *teaching to strength:* capitalizing on the oral language skills students already possess and helping students apply those skills immediately and effortlessly to writing" (1985, p. 290; [italics added]). Elbow and other L1 writing theorists have emphasized the use of oral language as a tool for writing, claiming that students should be encouraged to rely on their oral language knowledge for at least some of their writing (Bean et al., 2003; Bizzell, 1999; Elbow, 1985; Hebb, 2002; Szczepanski, 2003). Reduced to its essence, the L1 theorists' argument is that students' natural (i.e., speak- ing) voice is a legitimate platform from which to launch into academic writing and that expressive writing activities, such as journaling and freewriting, which tap the writer's spoken language, are legitimate tools for helping students bootstrap their way into more formal written registers.

The bootstrapping argument is an attractive one, and a num- ber of L2 writing theorists have adopted it (see e.g., Blanton, 1992, and Mangelsdorf, 1989). However, writing instructors are justified in viewing with skepticism the implication that what is valid for L1 writers is, ipso facto, valid for L2 writers as well. **How well, such skeptics may ask, can the dialogue approach be expected to work when the L2 students involved are those whose L2 oral language may not be considered, in Elbow's words, a "strength"?** Can a foreign student ESL writer like Oscar (see Chapter 3), whose oral skills in English are relatively weak compared to his writing ability, be expected to profit from activities that force him to fall back on his underdeveloped speaking voice? Or in the case of immigrant college ESL writers like Mauricio (see Chapter 6), whose spoken English is marked with the features of a non-standard dialect, won't relying on their oral knowledge of English virtually guarantee that they will at least initially produce written texts that are unacceptable to their professors?

And even if a more likely candidate is considered—an ESL writer like Francisco (also described in Chapter 3) whose oral fluency is stronger than his writing—the bootstrap argument still assumes that a learner's proficiency in one production modality (oral, in this case) will transfer positively to the other. L1 writing theorists may not question the validity of this assumption but, as Sperling and Freedman (2001) point out, we simply don't know enough about the nature of L2 writing proficiency to make such a claim with any assurance.

Yet, even given the individual proficiency asymmetries that exist among L2 writers, there is still a good case to be made for the dialogue approach, and that is the case for helping L2 writers to *find their voice*. In one sense, L2 writers and novice L1 writers are looking for the same thing: a personal style of written language that they can feel comfortable with, that they can easily tap, and that has enough range and flexibility to express their ideas. How does the dialogue approach help student writers develop a voice? Simply by providing them with more options. Writers searching for a voice are in a situation comparable to that of a shopper in the dressing room of a clothing store. In the process of discovering a comfortable voice, they "try on" a variety of different voices to see which one sounds best, as one might try on a new hat or a suit (Hebb,

2002; Michaels, 2005). In doing so, they experiment with all the options they have at their disposal: their L1 writing and speaking voices (Buell, 2004; Woodall, 2002), their L2 speaking voice (Sperling & Freedman, 2001), and their emerging L2 writing voice. Somewhere in this welter of voices they find one that suits them.

The previous chapter noted that some L2 writing theorists have discounted the importance of voice in L2 academic writing. However, from the dialogic perspective, voice is a critical element in a writer's development that cannot be ignored. Whether the writer's voice is a non-native version of the L2 or the voice of L1; whether it is a single loud voice or a jumble of contending voices, L2 writers, like all writers, must find a voice, or combination of voices, in which to express themselves (see excellent discussions on this issue in Braxley, 2005; Prior, 2001; Vitanova, 2005).

That voice may change over time as the L2 writer tries on different variants. This experimentation is an important part of literacy development; it's what novice L1 writers do when they first cast about for a formal writing voice—often settling first on an awkward version of academic prose so hopelessly "tied in knots that it is impenetrable" (Elbow, 1985, p. 291) before developing a more mature, robust, orally influenced style (see Chapter 2). Second language writers also need the chance to try out a variety of voices, which is precisely what happens when their instructors help them to tap their L2 oral proficiency through dialogic writing activities. Regardless of how weak or strong their conversational skills may be, writing with their oral voice enables L2 writers to widen their writing repertoires to include a broader range of available voices. If the student's oral voice is not as well developed as the written one, the dialogic writing classroom can help to strengthen both (Mangelsdorf, 1989).

What about Peer Response Groups?

No discussion of oral language in the teaching of L2 writers can ignore the issue of peer response activities in the classroom. Group and pair work, in which students provide feedback on each other's writing, are now common features of both L1 and L2 writing classrooms. However, Jessica Williams (2002) captures well the ambivalence among writing teachers and researchers over the value of this practice, referring to the "uneven effectiveness" of peer response (p. 80; see also Ferris & Hedgcock, 2005, for an excellent review of research in this area). In a volume in this series, *Peer Response in Second Language Writing Classrooms,* Liu and Hansen (2002), while generally promoting the use of peer group and pair work with L2 writers, readily acknowledge the skepticism, reservations, and logistical concerns that keep some writing teachers from including peer activities in their classes. The question then, is: **From the perspective of the dialogue approach, are writing teachers justified in asking their L2 writers to spend class time discussing their writing with classmates?**

A positive answer would seem to be a foregone conclusion. Of course, writing teachers who lean toward dialogic instruction would be more inclined to incorporate peer activities into their writing classes; after all, more interaction means more voices, resulting in more dialogue, especially with the teacher off center stage. And the arguments in the published literature in favor of peer response groups seem persuasive at first glance. Liu and Hansen (2002) cover in detail the claims that have been made for these activities, for both L1 and L2 writers, so they will only be briefly summarized here. The arguments in favor run as follows: First, peer feedback gives student writers a more highly developed **sense of audience,** since in group sessions they come face-to-face with their classmates' questions and confusions over aspects of their texts (Nystrand, 1986). Their classmates' queries help to highlight what is clear in their writing and what is not. Interaction with a real live audience helps novice writers to realize that while their texts may be clear to them, they aren't necessarily so to their readers. Writers are thus better able to assume a reader's perspective while drafting (Gere, 1990), and their resulting texts consequently display improved coherence (Sperling & Freedman, 2001; Stock & Robinson, 1990; Zebroski, 1994).

A second argument is that by discussing their texts with peers, student writers grow more **critically aware** of their own writing (Nystrand, 1986). As they discuss problems in other writers' papers, they become more sensitized to digressions and logical gaps in their own texts. And through in-depth discussion of texts with their peers, novice writers begin to develop a technical vocabulary (a writer's meta-language) with which to talk about writing (Gere, 1990). This argument seems no less persuasive for L2 writers than for native speakers.

Another claim made for peer response is the Vygotskian argument that discussing writing with other classmates leads to **increases in a learner's intellectual growth and cognitive development.** As previously noted, the sociocultural tradition holds that a learner's intellectual growth is rooted in social interaction. Thus, as L2 student writers interact with their classmates in pairs and groups, they have the opportunity to internalize the conversational give-and-take in the form of inner speech, a cognitive resource they can call on later to think through problems in planning and drafting texts (Anton & DiCamilla, 1998; Gere, 1990; Swain & Lapkin, 1998; Villamil & De Guerrero, 1996). A socioculturalist would also argue that when L2 writers work in pairs in which one student is more expert than the other, the ensuing conversations can result in **scaffolded learning,** an ideal kind of instructional discourse for non-native as well as native speakers (see Donato, 1994; Ohta, 2000, 2001; and Chapter 5 of this book for a full discussion).

A similar interactionist argument covered by Liu and Hansen (2002), and one directly applicable to L2 writers, holds that conversation in peer response groups promotes the **negotiation of meaning** among student participants. The small-group or pair format gives students more chances to "explain, defend and clarify" their texts (Villamil & De Guerrero, 1996, p. 69), and as students orally work through problems with their texts in groups or with partners, it is argued, they engage in clarification requests and responses, confirmation checks, and other types of conversational modifications that lead to enhanced L2 input (Williams, 2002, p. 82).

For advanced L2 writers in English for Academic Purposes (EAP) courses, the benefits of conversational negotiation may be particularly great. Liu and Hansen (2002) point out that when students work on their texts in groups with writers from other disciplines they must often rephrase and explain their written content so that their classmates can understand it. According to Liu and Hansen, the resulting discussion helps to clarify disciplinary knowledge in the student writer's own mind and to increase his or her flexibility in choosing among more and less technical L2 registers, depending on the sophistication of fellow group members (p. 53).

However persuasive these arguments may be, they have not gone unchallenged. Villamil and De Guerrero (1998) admit that the student pairs they studied did not always work together constructively—that some students did not actively participate at all, while others were dictatorial and tried to appropriate their fellow students' texts. Even in their generally favorable treatment of peer revision, Liu and Hansen (2002) are careful to point out that students do not always trust the comments of their peers and that they sometimes display "a lack of personal investment" in peer activities, making inappropriate comments and displaying off-task behavior (p. 53). Student peers are often distracted by local, mechanical errors in their classmates' writing at the expense of larger rhetorical or organizational concerns. It has also been suggested that cultural differences existing among some non-native speaker writers may work against building productive, collaborative revision groups in some classrooms (Carson & Nelson, 1994).

Where does all this leave us? The compatibility of peer response activities with the dialogue approach seems intuitive and logical, if not obvious. However, given the legitimate criticisms of group and pair work that have been raised, writing instructors have a responsibility to see that their L2 writers get as much benefit as possible from class time dedicated to peer writing activities. Thus, a few caveats are again in order.

- *First, we should ensure that group and pair work in our writing classes serve limited and well-defined instructional functions.* They are not an instructional panacea; there are obviously many cases where peer work is simply no substitute for the expert instruction and feedback of a teacher-fronted lesson (Villamil & De Guerrero, 1998).

- *Second, we should explain our rationale(s) for including these activities explicitly to our L2 writers, so that dubious students are less likely to see them as a waste of time.*
- *Third, we should examine critically the outcomes of specific types of peer activities by monitoring and assessing group work in our classes.* We may conclude, for example, that in some cases responding to other students' writing may be less effective for our L2 writers than are peer activities occurring at the initial planning stages of a writing assignment, where students can brainstorm in groups or pairs and help each other clarify the assignment.
- *To help students get the most out of the time they spend engaged in peer work, we should provide them with models of effective group discussion behavior and techniques* (Ferris & Hedgcock, 2005; Liu & Hansen, 2002).
- *We should establish clearly defined task objectives and procedural criteria for student groups so that they don't get bogged down in unproductive work.*
- *Finally, we must recognize that for L2 writers with weaker oral skills, or for those with a personal or cultural bias against classroom group work, peer writing activities simply may not achieve the desired objective.*

Anne Ruggles Gere has made the provocative claim that the quality of interaction observed in student writing groups is an index to "the quality of teaching that has gone before" (1990, p. 127). If that is indeed the case, it might be reason enough to include group work as a regular feature of writing instruction. And, given the current popularity of the process school of composition instruction and the prevalence of peer activities written into recently published L1 and L2 composition textbooks (see, e.g., the *Blueprints* texts and Swales & Feak, 2004), it is virtually inevitable that group and pair work will take up some part of nearly every L2 student writer's classroom time. It's the teacher's job to see that the time is well spent.

Dialogue and Responsibility

I have argued for the dialogue approach to teaching L2 writers as an effective and theoretically sound classroom pedagogy. There is more to dialogue, however, than theories of learning and teaching. Because dialogue puts students and teachers into close personal contact, there are personal and sometimes even ethical issues that may arise. To bring this critique to a close, we consider the larger implications of the dialogue approach—specifically, the kinds of relationships it encourages between teachers and students and the possible consequences of those relationships. The last question to be considered, then, is: **Are we as writing teachers prepared to take responsibility for the personal consequences of engaging with our students in dialogue?**

True dialogue (unlike dialectic) is unpredictable and to some degree ungovernable (Nystrand & Gamoran, 1991); thus, we are always in danger of learning more from, and about, our students than we may have bargained for. By removing barriers to our students' active participation and engaging them in an authentic and personal way, we invite them to tell us what they are thinking and feeling—about themselves, about what we are teaching them and about how we are teaching it, and about social issues in the world outside the classroom. This can sometimes lead to awkward and troubling situations.

Some examples are in order. As a writing teacher, my most striking moments of personal contact with students have come through journaling. Several years ago, in a series of journal entries, an older male L2 student confided to me details of his romantic relationships. I was taken aback and embarrassed by the forthrightness of some of his entries. Out of concern for my professional relationship with him, I felt obliged to steer our journal discussions to other topics. In another dialogue journal incident, I took a more directive approach, to my eventual regret. When a female student continually complained to me in her entries about the rudeness displayed toward her by North Americans, I wondered in one of my responses how her own attitudes and behavior have affected the people she met or her perceptions of them. She responded with an angry rejoinder that effectively ended our dialogue.

One semester during a recent presidential election I asked a sophisticated, older Mexican student through his journal to compare the rhetoric of our political campaigns with those in his country. He responded that no Mexican would be foolish enough to fall for a candidate's appeal to "family values." Again, though I did not disagree with the student's viewpoint, I felt defensive and angry that he had characterized voters in my country as gullible. It took me some time to regain a sympathetic attitude toward our journaling.

In a similar incident, while teaching EFL teachers-in-training in Europe during the run-up to the 2003 U.S. attack on Iraq, I was saddened to read in my students' journal entries how much they feared and disliked the United States as a world power. While I shared their disapproval of the war, I was taken aback by their perception of the United States as a malevolent force in the world. Even though I disagreed with my government's policies, I could not help but take such comments personally.

Such experiences are certainly not unique and perhaps no different from those of many writing teachers. They could conceivably occur whether or not it is L2 writers who are involved and whether or not the teacher deliberately employs a dialogic approach. The point is that by engaging students personally and encouraging them to communicate openly in their journals, in class discussions, and in conferencing, we openly invite personal response. In so doing, we virtually guarantee that students will raise, either orally in class or through their written communications, topics of personal concern to them. Once we let the dialogic cat out of the bag, so to speak, we must then be prepared to deal with it.

Through dialogue we and our students come to know each other as social beings better than we might in more traditionally organized classrooms, and we may not always feel comfortable with the people we come to know. We may learn that our students have a much greater level of expertise in certain areas than we do, a realization that may prove threatening to some, especially novice, teachers. We may learn what our students truly think about social issues outside the classroom, and what they think may not please us. For example, we may learn, as I have, that some of our students hold intolerant, stereotypical attitudes toward certain ethnic or religious groups. Although we may not always like the information they offer us in dialogue, and although we may not wish to pursue it, we do have the obligation to treat it, and them, responsibly.

In her book *On Austrian Soil,* Perl (2005a) deals with the personal consequences of teaching writing through dialogue in its starkest terms. Invited to teach a short course in composition research to Austrian teachers of English in Innsbruck, she found herself face-to-face with the personal histories of her students' families during World War II and with her own Jewish background. In the journals and conversation papers they read aloud to each other in class, she and her small group found themselves confronting past horrors, denial, and long hidden feelings. Because Perl dared to tell her students what she thought, they felt encouraged to do the same. The consequences were not trivial; she was accused of unprofessionalism by one of her students and cheered for her courage by others. In Perl's telling, the short course became a traumatic, though ultimately fulfilling, experience.

Perhaps this is the biggest risk we take in following the dialogue approach to teaching writing—the possibility that our classroom lessons will turn into unexpectedly significant social and personal events. The risk is always there, even in traditional, transmission style classrooms, but dialogue makes it all the more likely. As Perl (2005a) notes:

> Models of teaching that promote the teacher primarily or exclusively as a transmitter of information do not provide rich, interactive contexts for learning. Such contexts require intimacy, openness, mutual respect, trust and dialog. (p. 56)

As hinted at earlier, the key to dealing with the personal consequences of dialogue is **responsibility.** When we engage our students in dialogue, we charge ourselves with the responsibility for dealing with its consequences. When we create relationships of mutual trust with students, we take on the responsibility of treating them as real people and presenting ourselves as real people as well. As Perl (2005a) found out, this involves a moral responsibility as well as a professional one: "the ability and willingness to take another person's words and questions seriously. Not to turn our backs. Not to remain silent" (p. 84).

As Perl has said elsewhere (2005b), in our responses to students we must "respond responsibly." In other words, we are responsible for our own words and their consequences, and we share responsibility with our students to treat both sides of the dialogue seriously. As Hawisher and Selfe (1998) note, dialogic teaching

> involves an openness to the unknown and a rejection of stale or habitual approaches to education. To succeed in this kind of classroom…teachers must learn to become increasingly astute observers of students, students must learn to participate more actively and responsibly in their own education…all parties have to learn the importance of reflecting critically. (1998, p. ix)

When we engage in dialogue with writers from different cultures, first languages, and ethnic and national backgrounds, the chances are even greater that they will at one point or another delight, surprise, shock, or even dismay us with the comments they make or the questions they ask. The L2 writers in our classes may not share our cultural or personal values, or our assumptions about what constitutes socially appropriate discourse. When we experience this in conversation, oral or written, we may not like it, but we can't very well disparage, reject, or punish it since we have literally asked for it.

We should also be prepared for the possibility that some L2 writers, due to their cultural backgrounds or their own personalities, will resist our dialogic overtures. In the writing center they may not wish to take active part in class discussions; they may prefer to follow their tutor's advice at face value without actively participating in the tutorial conversation. They may prefer not to engage in written dialogue, and when they do, they may write superficially, keeping their true thoughts and feelings to themselves. We are also responsible for treating this choice with respect.

Dialogue as Parallel Pedagogy

Teaching writing, like teaching in any discipline, is a continuous process of making informed choices. Every instructor who works dialogically with L2 writers will most likely have to deal with the issues discussed here at one time or another, and each will choose to do so in his or her own way. To take the first issue, it must be recognized that dialogue is idiosyncratic; no outside observer or supervisor can script a teacher's oral style. Some teachers may prefer to engage in *dialectic* exchanges with their students rather than what might be considered a more natural conversational style. Over time, as dialogically inclined teachers become more conscious of their own oral styles, they will develop a personal version of instructional conversation that feels comfortable to them and seems well adapted to their students.

Regarding the second issue, no one can guarantee that tapping into L2 students' oral language through *group work* will pay off immediately with improvements in their writing or will work equally well for all students. A more reasonable expectation is that peer activities may awaken some students to the possibilities and resources residing in their oral language abilities and may prompt them as writers to become more sensitive to the needs of their readers. Every teacher must make informed choices about when and how best to incorporate group work in his or her writing lessons, if at all.

And most certain, no one can predict into what *personal territory* the dialogue between a particular instructor and a particular class or writer, L1 or L2, may lead. Teachers who choose to incorporate a dialogue approach must learn to expect the unexpected and to exploit in their own ways every turn in the conversation, no matter how unpromising or confrontational, as a pedagogical opportunity for the improvement of writing. In sum, dialogic pedagogy must be reinvented by each teacher making new choices with each new L2 student writer.

One choice may be to temporarily abandon the dialogic approach. As acknowledged previously, dialogue-based activities do not serve all L2 writers equally well at all points in their writing development. And teaching dialogically may prove impractical for some teachers in some instructional situations—for example, with a group of students who can't or won't participate constructively or in institutions where teachers are enjoined from what might be perceived as "teaching away from the textbook." In such cases teachers are justified in choosing to turn from dialogic engagement to more traditional, recitation-style instruction.

But such situation-specific choices do not constitute an indictment of the dialogue approach. On the contrary, L2 students' written and oral proficiencies should both benefit from a pedagogy that includes both. As I and others have argued, the writing classroom is as legitimate a place as any other for language acquisition to occur and to be encouraged (Harklau, 2002; Reichelt, 1999; Weissberg, 2000). If an unforeseen outcome of dialogic instruction is that students acquire a higher level of general L2 competence (Ellis, 1994; White, 2003), so much the better; a rising tide of general language competence should raise the learner's performance levels in all language skills, including writing.

The preceding chapters have looked at theories that underlie incorporating dialogue into teaching L2 writers and have argued for specific techniques to implement dialogic teaching. However, it must be clarified in closing that dialogue is not so much a teaching method, a tool kit of techniques, or even an approach. It is more than anything an attitude—an attitude about the nature of writing, the nature of teaching, and in this particular case, the nature of L2 learning. It is an attitude that, at its core, recognizes that what works best for writers in the classroom is no different from what works best for writers in other spheres of social activity. Because nearly all writing in the world beyond the classroom is embedded in writers' social activities and experiences, the best writing pedagogy should be the one that brings that reality into the classroom (Rabkin & Smith, 1990). By infusing our writing classes with oral language at as many points in the instructional scheme as possible, we mirror that same reality for our L2 writers. Writing instruction, like writing itself, is a social activity and that is why dialogue about writing is imperative.

Discussion Questions

1. In your experiences either as a writing teacher or as a student, what **awkward personal or social situations** has classroom dialogue led to? In your opinion, were the teachers in these situations able to turn the awkwardness or confrontation to pedagogical advantage in terms of students' writing?

2. Have you been in a classroom where the instructor's verbal style **actively discouraged dialogue** with (or among) students? What specific elements of the instructor's discourse do you think might have been responsible for creating this atmosphere?

3. In your view, when might dialogic instruction be **inappropriate**?

4. The dialogic approach to teaching L2 writers described here assumes that L2 proficiency in writing and speaking are not totally separate constructs, that is, that they are connected by some **underlying or general L2 proficiency** that affects, and is affected by, development in either of the two production modalities. What evidence is there to support this view? What arguments have been made by applied linguists against it? How could this assumption be tested?

References

Aljaafreh, A., & Lantolf, J. (1994). Negative feedback as regulation and second language learning in the zone of proximal development. *Modern Language Journal, 78*(4), 465–483.

Anson, C. (1999). Talking about text: The use of recorded commentary in response to student writing. In R. Staub (Ed.), *A sourcebook for responding to student writing* (pp. 165–174). Cresskill, NJ: Hampton Press.

Anton, M., & DiCamilla, F. (1998). Socio-cognitive functions on L1 collaborative interaction in the L2 classroom. *Canadian Modern Language Review, 54.* Available: http://www.utpjournals.com/product/cmlr/543/543-Anton.html

Barnes, D. (1990). Oral language and learning. In S. Hynds & D. Rubin (Eds.), *Perspectives on talk and learning* (pp. 41–54). Urbana, IL: National Council of Teachers of English.

Barton, E. (2004). Linguistic discourse analysis: How the language in texts works. In C. Bazerman & P. Prior (Eds.), *What writing does and how it does it* (pp. 57–82). Mahwah, NJ: Lawrence Erlbaum.

Bates, L., Lane, J., & Lange, E. (1993). *Writing clearly: Responding to ESL compositions.* Boston: Heinle & Heile.

Bawarshi, A., & Pelkowski, S. (1999). Postcolonialism and the idea of a writing center. *The Writing Center Journal, 19,* 41–58.

Bean, J., Eddy, R., Grego, R., Irvine, P., Kutz, E., Matsuda, P., Cucchiara, M., Elbow, P., Haswell, R., Kennedy E., & Lehner, A. (2003). Should we invite students to write in home languages? Complicating the yes/no debate. *Composition Studies, 31,* 25–42.

Beauvois, M., & Eledge, J. (1996). Personality types and megabytes: Student attitudes toward computer mediated communication (CMC) in the language classroom. *CALICO Journal, 13,* 27–45.

Belcher, D. (1999). Authentic interaction in a virtual classroom: Leveling the playing field in a graduate seminar. *Computers and Composition, 16,* 253–267.

Bereiter, C., & Scardamalia, M. (1982). From conversation to composition: The role of instruction in a developmental process. In R. Glaser (Ed.), *Advances in instructional psychology: Vol. 2* (pp. 1–64). Hillsdale, NJ: Lawrence Erlbaum.

Berzsenyi, C. (1999). Teaching interlocutor relationships in electronic classrooms. *Computers & Composition, 16,* 229–247.

Berzsenyi, C. (2000). How to conduct a course-based computer chat room. *Teaching English in the Two-Year College, 28,* 165–174.

Berzsenyi, C. (2001). Comments to comments: Teachers and students in written dialog about critical revision. *Composition Studies, 29,* 71–92.

Bizzell, P. (1999). Hybrid academic discourses: What, why, how. *Composition Studies, 27,* 7–21.

Blanton, L. (1992). Talking students into writing: Using oral fluency to develop literacy. *TESOL Journal, 1,* 23–26.

Blau, S., & Hall, J. (2002). Guilt-free tutoring: Rethinking how we tutor nonnative English speaking students. *The Writing Center Journal, 23,* 23–44.

Bloch, J. (2002). Student/teacher interacation via email: The social context of Internet discourse. *Journal of Second Language Writing, 11,* 117–134.

Boyd, M., & Maloof, V. (2000). How teachers can build on student-proposed intertextual links to facilitate student talk in the ESL classroom. In J. Hall & L. Verplaetse (Eds.), *Second and foreign language learning through classroom interaction* (pp. 163–182). Mahwah, NJ: Lawrence Erlbaum.

Boyd, M., & Rubin, D. (2002). Elaborated student talk in an elementary ESOL classroom. *Research in the Teaching of English, 36,* 495–530.

Brannon, L., & Knoblauch, C. (1982). On students' rights to their own texts: A model of teacher response. *College Composition and Communication, 33,* 157–166.

Braxley, K. (2005). Mastering academic English: International graduate students' use of dialog and speech genres to meet the writing demands of graduate school. In J. Hall, G. Vitanova, & L. Marchenkova (Eds.), *Dialogue with Bakhtin on second and foreign language learning: New perspectives* (pp. 11–32). Mahwah, NJ: Lawrence Erlbaum.

Britton, J. (1970). *Language and learning.* Harmondsworth, UK: Pelican Books.

Britton, J., Burgess, T., Martin, N., McLeod, A., & Rosen, H. (1975). *The development of writing abilities (11–18)*. Houndsmills, U.K.: Macmillan.

Brookfield, S., & Preskill, S. (1999). *Discussion as a way of teaching: Tools and techniques for democratic classrooms*. San Francisco: Jossey-Bass.

Brooks, J. (1991). Minimalist tutoring: Making the student do all the work. *Writing Lab Newsletter 15*(6): 1–4.

Bruffee, K. (1995). Peer tutoring and the "conversation of mankind." In C. Murphy & J. Law (Eds.), *Landmark essays on writing centers* (pp. 87–98). Davis, CA: Hermagoras Press.

Bruffee, K. (1999). *Collaborative learning: Higher education, independence, and the authority of knowledge* (2nd ed.). Baltimore: Johns Hopkins University Press.

Bruffee, K. (2002). Collaboration, conversation and reacculturation. In G. DeLuca, L. Fox, M. Johnson, & M. Kogen (Eds.), *Dialog on writing: Rethinking ESL, basic writing and first-year composition* (pp. 63–81). Mahwah, NJ: Lawrence Erlbaum.

Buell, M. (2004). Code-switching and second language writing: How multiple codes are combined in text. In C. Bazerman & P. Prior (Eds.), *What writing does and how it does it* (pp. 97–122). Mahwah, NJ: Lawrence Erlbaum.

Carson, J., & Nelson, G. (1994). Writing groups: Cross-cultural issues. *Journal of Second Language Writing, 3*, 17–30.

Cazden, C. (1988). *Classroom discourse: The language of teaching and learning*. Portsmouth, NH: Heinemann.

Chafe, W. (1982). Integration and involvement in speaking, writing and oral literature. In D. Tannen (Ed.), *Spoken and writing language: Exploring orality and literacy* (pp. 35–54). Norwood, NJ: Ablex.

Clay, M. (1991). *Becoming literate: The construction of inner control*. Portsmouth, NH: Heinemann.

Coffin, C., & Hewings, A. (2005). Engaging electronically: Using CMC to develop students' argumentation skills in higher education. *Language and Education, 19*, 32–49.

Colombi, C. (2002). Academic language development in Latino students' writing in Spanish. In M. Schleppegrell & M. Colombi (Eds.), *Developing advanced literacy in first and second languages: Meaning with power* (pp. 67–86). Mahwah, NJ: Lawrence Erlbaum.

Cumming, A. (1989). Writing expertise and second-language proficiency. *Language Learning, 39*, 81–141.

Cumming, A. (1992). Instructional routines in ESL composition teaching: A case study of three teachers. *Journal of Second Language Writing, 1,* 17–35.

De Guerrero, M., & Villamil, O. (2000). Activating the ZPD: Mutual scaffolding in peer revision. *Modern Language Journal, 84*, 51–68.

DeLuca, G., Fox, L., Johnson, M., & Kogen, M. (Eds.) (2002). *Dialogue on writing: Rethinking ESL, basic writing and first-year composition*. Mahwah, NJ: Lawrence Erlbaum.

Dickinson, D., Wolf, M., & Stotsky, S. (1993). Words move: The interwoven development of oral and written language. In J. Gleason (Ed.), *The development of language* (pp. 369–420). New York: Macmillan.

Doerfler, T., & Davis, R. (1998). Conferencing in the contact zone. In J. Galin & J. Latchaw (Eds.), *The dialogic classroom: Teachers integrating computer technology, pedagogy and research* (pp. 174–190). Urbana, IL: National Council of Teachers of English.

Donato, R. (1994). Collective scaffolding in second language learning. In J. Lantolf & G. Appel (Eds.), *Vygotskian approaches to second language research* (pp. 33–56). Norwood, NJ: Ablex.

Dyson, A. (1988). Talking up a writing community: The role of talk in learning to write. In S. Hynds & D. Rubin (Eds.), *Perspectives on talk and learning* (pp. 99–114). Urbana, IL: National Council of Teachers of English.

Dyson, A. (1995). Writing children: Reinventing the development of childhood literacy. *Written Communication, 12*, 4–46.

Dyson, A. (2000). Linking writing and community development through the children's forum. In C. Lee & P. Smagorinsky (Eds.), *Vygotskian perspectives on literacy research: Constructing knowledge through collaborative inquiry* (pp. 127–149). Cambridge: Cambridge University Press.

Elbow, P. (1985). The shifting relationships between speech and writing. *College Composition and Communication, 36*, 283–303.

Elbow, P. (2002). High stakes and low stakes in assigning and responding to writing. In G. DeLuca et al. (Eds.), *Dialog on writing: Rethinking ESL, basic writing and first-year composition* (pp. 289–298). Mahwah, NJ: Lawrence Erlbaum.

Ellis, R. (1994). *The study of second language acquisition*. Amsterdam: John Benjamins.

Ellis, R. (1999). *Learning a second language through interaction.* Amsterdam: John Benjamins.

Ferris, D. (2002). *Treatment of error in second language student writing.* Ann Arbor: University of Michigan Press.

Ferris, D. (2003). *Response to student writing: Implications for second language students.* Mahwah, NJ: Lawrence Erlbaum.

Ferris, D., & Hedgcock, J. (2005). *Teaching ESL composition: Purpose, process and practice* (2nd ed.). Mahwah, NJ: Lawrence Erlbaum.

Ferris, D., Pezone, S., Tade, C., & Tiniti, S. (1997). Teacher commentary on student writing: Descriptions and implications. *Journal of Second Language Writing, 6,* 155–182.

Flanders, N. (1970). *Analyzing teaching behavior.* Reading, MA: Addison-Wesley.

Galin, J., & Latchaw, J. (1998). *The dialogic classroom: Teachers integrating computer technology, pedagogy and research.* Urbana, IL: National Council of Teachers of English.

Gay, P. (1998). Dialogizing response in the writing classroom: Students answer back. *Journal of Basic Writing, 17,* 3–17.

Gere, A. (1990). Talking in writing groups. In S. Hynds & D. Rubin (Eds.), *Perspectives on talk and learning* (pp. 115–128). Urbana, IL: National Council of Teachers of English.

Gillam, A. (1991). Writing center ecology: A Bakhtinian perspective. *The Writing Center Journal, 11,* 3–12.

Goldenberg, C. (1993). Instructional conversations: Promoting comprehension through discussion. *The Reading Teacher, 46,* 316–326.

Goldstein, L. (2004). Questions and answers about teacher written commentary and student revision: Teachers and students working together. *Journal of Second Language Writing 13,* 63–80.

Goldstein, L. (2005). *Teacher written commentary in second language writting classrooms.* Ann Arbor: University of Michigan Press.

Goldstein, L., & Conrad, S. (1990). Student input and negotiation of meaning in ESL writing conferences. *TESOL Quarterly, 24,* 433–460.

Grabill, J. (1994). Tutor and ESL student oral communication in the writing center: An inquiry into strategies for effective tutoring. *The Writing Lab Newsletter, 19,* 8–11.

Grice, H. (1975). Logic and conversation. In P. Cole & J. Morgan (Eds.), *Speech acts* (pp. 41–58). New York: Academic Press.

Gutierrez, K. (1994). How talk, context and script shape contexts for learning: A cross-case comparison of journal sharing. *Linguistics and Education, 5*, 335–365.

Hall, J., & Verplaetse, L. (Eds.). (2000). *Second and foreign language learning through classroom interaction* (Introduction). Mahwah, NJ: Lawrence Erlbaum.

Hall, J., Vitanova, G., & Marchenkova, L. (Eds.) (2005). *Dialogue with Bakhtin on second and foreign language learning.* Mahwah, NJ: Lawrence Erlbaum.

Halliday, M. (1987). Spoken and written modes of meaning. In R. Horowitz & S. Samuels (Eds.), *Comprehending oral and written language* (pp. 55–82). San Diego: Academic Press.

Halliday, M. (1989). *Spoken and written language.* Oxford: Oxford University Press.

Hamilton, W. (1973) (translator). *Plato's Phaedrus and the seventh and eighth letters.* London: Penguin Books.

Harklau, L. (1999). Representing culture in the ESL writing classroom. In E. Hinkle (Ed.), *Culture in second language teaching and learning* (pp. 109–130). Cambridge: Cambridge University Press.

Harklau, L. (2002). The role of writing in classroom second language acquisition. *Journal of Second Language Writing, 11*, 329–350.

Harklau, L., Losey, K., & Siegal, M. (Eds). (1999). *Generation 1.5 meets college composition: Issues in the teaching of writing to U.S.-educated learners of ESL.* Mahwah, NJ: Lawrence Erlbaum.

Harris, M. (1986). *Teaching one-to-one: The writing conference.* Urbana, IL: National Council of Teachers of English.

Harris, M. (1990). Teacher/student talk: The collaborative conference. In S. Hynds & D. Rubin (Eds.), *Perspectives on talk and learning* (pp. 149–161). Urbana, IL: National Council of Teachers of English.

Harris, M. (1995). Talking in the middle: Why writers need tutors. *College English, 57*, 27–42.

Hawisher, G., & Selfe, C. (1998). Forward. In J. Galin & J. Latchaw (Eds.), *The dialogic classroom: Teachers integrating computer technology, pedagogy and research* (pp. vii–x). Urbana, IL: National Council of Teachers of English.

Hebb, J. (2002). Mixed forms of academic discourse: A continuum of language possibility. *Journal of Basic Writing, 21*, 21–36.

Hedgcock, J., & Lefkowitz, N. (1992). Collaborative oral/aural revision in foreign language writing instruction. *Journal of Second Language Writing, 1,* 255–276.

Hewitt, B. (forthcoming). A study of synchronous whiteboard instruction. *Computers and Composition, 23,* 4–31.

Hirvela, A. (1999). Collaborative writing instruction and communities of readers and writers. *TESOL Journal,* 7–12.

Holdaway, D. (1984). *The foundations of literacy.* Southam, UK: Scholastic.

Hudelson, S. (2005). Taking on English writing in a bilingual program: Revisiting, reexamining, reconceptualizing the data. In P. Matsuda & T. Silva (Eds.), *Second language research: Perspectives on the process of knowledge construction* (pp. 207–220). Mahwah, NJ: Lawrence Erlbaum.

Jackson, R. (2002). Writing center consultations. In D. Roen, V. Pantoja, L. Yena, S.K. Miller, & E. Waggoner (Eds.), *Strategies for teaching first year composition* (pp. 372–385). Urbana, IL: National Council of Teachers of English.

John-Steiner, V., & Mahn, H. (1996). Sociocultural approaches to learning and development: A Vygotskian framework. *Educational Psychologist, 31,* 191–206.

Kantor, K., & Rubin, D. (1981). Between speaking and writing: Processes of differentiation. In B. Kroll & R. Vann (Eds.) (pp. 55–81). *Exploring speaking/writing relationships: Connections and contrasts.* Urbana, IL: National Council of Teachers of English.

Kemp, F. (1998). Computer-mediated communication: Making nets work for writing instruction. In J. Galin & J. Latchaw (Eds.), *The dialogic classroom: Teachers integrating computer technology, pedagogy and research* (pp. 133–150). Urbana, IL: National Council of Teachers of English.

Knoblauch, C., & Brannon, L. (1981). Teacher commentary on student writing: The state of the art. *Freshman English News, 10,* 1–4.

Knoblauch, C., & Brannon, L. (2002). Responding to texts: Facilitating revision in the writing workshop. In G. DeLuca, L. Fox, M. Johnson, & M. Kogen (Eds.), *Dialog on writing: Rethinking ESL, basic writing and first-year composition* (pp. 251–269). Mahwah, NJ: Lawrence Erlbaum.

Krashen, S. (1981). *Second language acquisition and second language learning.* Oxford: Pergamon Press.

Kroll, B. (1981). Developmental relationships in speaking and writing. In B. Kroll & R. Vann (Eds.) (pp. 32–54). *Exploring speaking/writing relationships: Connections and contrasts.* Urbana, IL: National Council of Teachers of English.

Kroll, B., & Vann, R. (1981). (Eds.) *Exploring speaking-writing relationships: Connections and contrasts.* Urbana, IL: National Council of Teachers of English.

Lantolf, J. (Ed.) (2000). *Sociocultural theory and second language learning.* Cambridge: Cambridge University Press.

Lantolf, J., & Appel G. (Eds.) (1994). *Vygotskian approaches to second language acquisition.* Norwood, NJ: Ablex.

Lee C., & Smagorinsky, P. (2000). *Vygotskian perspectives on literacy research: Constructing meaning through collaborative inquiry.* Cambridge: Cambridge University Press.

Leki, I. (1992). *Understanding ESL writers: A guide for teachers.* Portsmouth, NH: Boynton/Cook Heinemann.

Leont'yev, A. (1969). Inner speech and the processes of grammatical generation of utterances. *Soviet Psychology, 7*, 11–16.

Lillis, T. (2003). Student writing as "academic literacies": Drawing on Bakhtin to move from critique to design. *Language Education, 17*, 192–207.

Liu, J., & Hansen, J. (2002). *Peer response in second language writing classrooms.* Ann Arbor: University of Michigan Press.

Loomis, O. (2003). From oral narratives to written essays. In W. Bishop (Ed.), *The subject is writing: Essays by teachers and students* (pp. 53–62). Portsmouth, NH: Boynton/Cook Heinemann.

Luria, A. (1969). Speech development and the formation of mental processes. In M. Cole & I. Maltzman (Eds.), *A handbook of contemporary Soviet psychology* (pp. 121–162). New York: Basic Books.

McCafferty, S. (1992). The use of private speech by adult second language learners: A cross-cultural study. *Modern Language Journal, 76*, 179–189.

McCafferty, S. (1994). The use of private speech by adult ESL learners at different levels of proficiency. In J. Lantolf & G. Appel (Eds.), *Vygotskian approaches to second language research* (pp.117–134). Norwood, NJ: Ablex.

McCloskey, D. (2000). *Economical writing* (2nd ed.). Prospect Heights, NJ: Waveland Press.

Mangelsdorf, K. (1989). Parallels between speaking and writing in second language acquisition. In D. Johnson & D. Roen (Eds.), *Richness in writing: Empowering ESL students* (pp. 134–145). New York: Longman.

Mangelsdorf, K., & Schlumberger, S. (1992). ESL student response stances in a peer-review task. *Journal of Second Language Writing, 1*, 235–254.

Mantero, M. (2002). Evaluating classroom communication: In support of emergent and authentic frameworks in second language assessment. *Practical Assessment, Research & Evaluation, 10.* Available: http://pareonline.net/getvn.asp?v=8&n=8

Mehan, H. (1985). The structure of classroom discourse. In T. Van Dijk (Ed.), *Handbook of discourse analysis: Vol. 3* (pp. 119–131). London: Academic Press.

Menasche, L. (1997). *Writing a research paper* (rev. ed.). Ann Arbor: University of Michigan Press.

Michaels, A. (2005, March). *Entering the conversation: Using hybrid discourses in the composition classroom.* Paper presented at the College Conference on Composition and Communication, San Francisco.

Moll, L. (1989). Teaching second language students: A Vygotskian perspective. In D. Johnson & D. Roen (Eds.), *Richness in writing: Empowering ESL students* (pp. 55–69). New York: Longman.

Moll, L. (Ed.) (1990). *Vygotsky and education: Instructional implications and applications of sociohistorical psychology.* Cambridge: Cambridge University Press.

Myers, S. (2003). Reassessing the "proofreading trap": ESL tutoring and writing instruction. *The Writing Center Journal, 24*, 51–70.

Nightingale, A. (1995). *Genres in dialog: Plato and the construct of philosophy.* Cambridge: Cambridge University Press.

North, S. (1984). The idea of a writing center. *College English, 46*, 433–446.

Nunan, D. (1999). *Second language teaching and learning.* Boston: Heinle & Heinle.

Nystrand, M. (1986). Learning to write by talking about writing. In N. Nystrand (Ed.), The structure of written communication (pp. 179–211). Orlando, FL: Academic Press.

Nystrand, M. (1997). *Opening dialog: Understanding the dynamics of language and learning in the English classroom.* New York: Teachers College Press.

Nystrand, M., & Gamoran, A. (1991). Student engagement: When recitation becomes conversation. In H. C. Waxman & H. Walberg (Eds.), *Effective teaching: Current research* (pp. 257–276). Berkeley, CA: McCutchan.

Ohta, A. (1995). Applying sociocultural theory to an analysis of learner discourse: Learner-learner collaborative interaction in the zone of proximal development. *Issues in Applied Linguistics, 6,* 93–121.

Ohta, A. (2000). Rethinking interaction in SLA: Developmentally appropriate assistance in the zone of proximal development and the acquisition of L2 grammar. In J. Lantolf (Ed.), *Sociocultural theory and second language learning.* Oxford: Oxford University Press.

Ohta, A. (2001). *Second language acquisition processes in the classroom.* Mahwah, NJ: Lawrence Erlbaum.

Olson, D. (1977). From utterance to text: The bias of language in speech and writing. *Harvard Educational Review, 47*(3), 257–281.

Onore, C. (1990). Negotiation, language and inquiry: Building knowledge collaboratively in the classroom. In S. Hynds & D. Rubin (Eds.), *Perspectives on talk and learning* (pp. 57–72). Urbana, IL: National Council of Teachers of English.

Palinscar, A. (1986). The role of dialog in providing scaffolded instruction. *Educational Psychologist, 21,* 73–98.

Palinscar, A., & Brown, A. (1984). Reciprocal teaching of comprehension-fostering and comprehension-monitoring activities. *Cognition and Instruction, 1,* 117–175.

Patthey-Chavez, G., & Ferris, D. (1997). Writing conferences and weaving of multi-voiced texts in college composition. *Research in the Teaching English, 31,* 51–90.

Pavlenko, A., & Lantolf, J. (2000). Second language learning as participation and the (re)construction of selves. In J. Lantolf (Ed.), *Sociocultural theory and second language learning* (pp. 155–178). Oxford: Oxford University Press.

Perl, S. (2005a). *On Austrian soil: Teaching those I was taught to hate.* Albany, NY: State University of New York Press.

Perl, S. (2005b, March). *Breaking the cycle of hate: a teacher's journey.* Paper presented at the 56th annual College Conference on Composition and Communication, San Francisco.

Peyton, J., & Reed, L. (1990). *Dialogue journal writing with nonnative English speakers: A handbook for teachers.* Alexandria, VA: Teachers of English to Speakers of Other Languages.

Phelps, L. (1989). Images of student writing: The deep structure of teacher response. In C. Anson (Ed.), *Writing and response: Theory, practice and research* (pp. 37–67). Urbana, IL: National Council of Teachers of English.

Powers, J. (1993). Rethinking writing center conferencing strategies for the ESL writer. *Writing Center Journal, 13,* 39–47.

Prior, P. (2001). Voices in text, mind, and society: Sociohistoric accounts of discourse acquisition and use. *Journal of Second Language Writing, 10,* 55–81.

Rabkin, E., & Smith, M. (1990). *Teaching writing that works: A group approach to practical English.* Ann Arbor: University of Michigan Press.

Rafoth, B. (2004). Tutoring ESL papers online. In S. Bruce & B. Rafoth (Eds.), *ESL writers: A guide for writing center tutors* (pp. 94–104). Portsmouth, NH: Boynton/Cook Heinemann.

Ramanathan, V., & Atkinson, D. (1999). Individualism, academic writing and ESL writers. *Journal of Second Language Writing, 8,* 55–81.

Rankin, E. (2001). *The work of writing.* San Francisco: Jossey-Bass.

Reichelt, M. (1999). Toward a more comprehensive view of L2 writing: Foreign language writing in the U.S. *Journal of Second Language Writing, 8,* 181–204.

Reid, J. (1994). *The process of paragraph writing* (2nd ed.). Englewood Cliffs, NJ: Prentice Hall Regents.

Reid, J. (1998). "Eye" learners and "ear" learners: Identifying the language needs of international student and U.S. resident writers. In P. Byrd & J. Reid (Eds.), *Grammar in the composition classroom: Essays on teaching ESL for college-bound students* (pp. 3–17). Boston: Heinle & Heinle.

Reid, J. (2002). Teaching composition to speakers of other languages. In L. Troyka, *Simon & Schuster handbook for writers* (pp. AIE-28—AIE-37). Upper Saddle River, NJ: Prentice Hall.

Robertson, M. (1986). Is anybody listening?: Responding to student writing. *College Composition and Communication, 37,* 87–91.

Roebuck, R. (2000). Subjects speak out: How learners position themselves in a psycholinguistic task. In J. Lantolf (Ed.), *Sociocultural theory and second language learning* (pp. 79–96). Oxford: Oxford University Press.

Rubin, D. (1988). Ways of talking about talking and learning. In S. Hynds & D. Rubin (Eds.), *Perspectives on talk and learning* (pp. 1–17). Urbana, IL: National Council of Teachers of English.

Rubin, D., & Dodd, W. (1987). *Talking into writing: Exercises for basic writ-ers*. Urbana, IL: National Council of Teachers of English.

Rubin, D., Goodrum, R., & Hall, B. (1990). Orality, oral-based culture, and the academic writing of ESL learners. *Issues in Applied Linguistics, 1,* 57–76.

Rubin, D., & Kantor, K. (1984). Talking and writing: Building communication competence. In C. Thaiss & C. Suhor (Eds.), *Speaking and writing* (pp. 29–74). Urbana, IL: National Council of Teachers of English.

Scane, J., Guy, A., & Wenstrom, L. (1994). *Think, write, share: Process writing for adult ESL and basic education students*. San Diego: Dominie Press.

Shuy, R. (1987). Dialog as the heart of learning. *Language Arts, 64,* 890–897.

Slobin, D. (1996). From "thought and language" to "thinking for speaking." In J. Gumperz & S. Levinson (Eds.), *Rethinking linguistic relativity* (pp. 70–96). Cambridge: Cambridge University Press.

Sperling, M. (1991). Dialogues of deliberation: Conversation in the teacher-student writing conference. *Written Communication, 8,* 131–162.

Sperling, M., & Freedman, S. (2001). Review of writing research. In V. Richardson (Ed.), *Handbook of research on teaching* (4th ed.), pp. 370–389. Washington, DC: American Education Research Association.

Stock, P., & Robinson, J. (1990). Literacy as conversation: Classroom talk as text building. In J. Robinson (Ed.), *Conversations on the written word: Essays on language and literacy* (pp. 163–238). Portsmouth, NH: Boyton/Cook Publishers.

Straub, R. (1999). The concept of control. In R. Straub (Ed.), *A sourcebook for responding to student writing,* (pp. 128–152). Cresskill, NJ: Hampton Press, Inc.

Swain, M. (1985). Communicative Competence: Some roles of comprehensible input and comprehensible output in its development. In S. Gass & C. Madden (Eds.), *Input in second language acquisition* (pp. 235–253). Rowley, MA: Newbury House.

Swain, M., & Lapkin, S. (1998). Interaction and second language learning: Two adolescent French immersion students working together. *Modern Language Journal, 82,* 320–337.

Swain, M., & Lapkin, S. (2001). Focus on form through collaborative dialogue: Exploring task effects. In M. Bygate, P. Skehan, & M. Swain (Eds.), *Researching pedagogic tasks: Second language learning, teaching and testing* (pp. 99–118). London: Longman.

Swales, J., & Feak, C. (2004). *Academic writing for graduate students: Essential tasks and skills* (2nd ed.). Ann Arbor: University of Michigan Press.

Szczepanski, J. (2003). Hearing voices: Yours, mine, others. In W. Bishop (Ed.), *The subject is writing* (pp. 210–219). Portsmouth, NH: Boynton/ Cook Heinemann.

Tannen, D. (1985). Relative focus on involvement in oral and written discourse. In D. Olson, N. Torrance, & A. Hildyard (Eds.), *Literacy, language and learning: The nature and consequences of reading and writing* (pp. 124–147). Cambridge: Cambridge University Press.

Tharp, R., & Entz, S. (2003). From high chair to high school: Research-based principles for teaching complex thinking. *Young Children, 58*, 38–44.

Tharp, R., & Gallimore, R. (1988). *Rousing minds to life.* Cambridge: Cambridge University Press.

Tharp, R., & Gallimore, R. (1991). *The Instructional Conversation: Teaching and Learning in Social Activity* (Research Report No. 2). Santa Cruz, CA: National Center for Research on Cultural Diversity and Second Language Learning.

Thonus, T. (1993). Tutors as teachers: Assisting ESL/EFL students in the writing center. *Writing Center Journal, 13*, 13–26.

Thonus, T. (1999a). *NS–NNS interaction in academic writing tutorials: Discourse analysis and its interpretations.* Paper presented at meeting of American Association of Applied Linguistics, Stamford, CT.

Thonus, T. (1999b). How to communicate politely and be a tutor too: NS-NSS interaction and writing center practice. *Text, 19*, 253–279.

Valdez, G., Haro, P., & Echevarriarza, M. (1992). The development of writing abilities in a foreign language: Contributions toward a general theory of L2 writing. *The Modern Language Journal, 76*, 333–352.

Vann, R. (1981). Bridging the gap between oral and written communication in EFL. In B. Kroll & R. Vann (Eds.), *Exploring speaking-writing relationships: Connections and contrasts* (pp. 154–177). Urbana, IL: National Council of Teachers of English.

Villamil, O., & De Guerrero, M. (1996). Peer revision in the L2 classroom: Social-cognitive activities, mediating strategies, and aspects of social behavior. *Journal of Second Language Writing, 5*, 51–73.

Villamil, O., & De Guerrero, M. (1998). Assesing the impact of peer revsion on L2 writing. *Applied Linguistics, 19*, 491–514.

Vitanova, G. (2005). Authoring the self in a non-native language: A dialogic approach to agency and subjectivity. In J. Hall, G. Vitanova, & L. Marchenkova (Eds.), *Dialogue with Bakhtin on second and foreign language learning: New perspectives* (pp. 149–169). Mahwah, NJ: Lawrence Erlbaum.

Vygotsky, L. (1986). *Thought and language.* Cambridge, MA: MIT Press.

Weissberg, R. (1994). Speaking of writing: Some functions of talk in the ESL composition class. *Journal of Second Language Writing, 3,* 121–139.

Weissberg, R. (1998). Acquiring English syntax through journal writing. *College ESL, 8,* 1–22.

Weissberg, R. (2000). Developmental relationships in the acquisition of English syntax: writing vs. speech. *Learning and Instruction, 10,* 37–53.

Weissberg, R. (2006). Scaffolded feedback: Conversations with advanced L2 writers. In K. Hyland & F. Hyland (Eds.), *Feedback in second language writing: Contexts and themes.* Cambridge: Cambridge University Press.

Weissberg, R., & Lipoufski, M. (2002). Borders and barriers: A model for a local issues ESL course. *TESOL Journal, 11*(2), 12–18.

Wells, G. (1990). Talk about text: Where literacy is learned and taught. *Curriculum Inquiry, 20,* 369–405.

Wells, G. (1993). Reevaluating the IRF sequence: A proposal for the articulation of theories of activity and discourse for the analysis of teaching and learning in the classroom. *Linguistics and Education, 5,* 1–37.

Wells, G. (2000). Dialogic inquiry in education: Building on the legacy of Vygotsky. In C. Lee & P. Smagorinsky (Eds.), *Vygotskian Perspectives on literacy research: Constructing meaning through collaborative inquiry* (pp. 51–85). Cambridge: Cambridge University Press.

Wells, G., & Chang-Wells, G.L. (1992). *Constructing knowledge together: Classrooms as centers of inquiry and literacy.* Portsmouth, NH: Heinemann.

Wertsch, J. (1991). *Voices of the mind: A socio-cultural approach to mediated action.* Cambridge, MA: Harvard University Press.

White, L. (2003). *Second language acquisition and universal grammar.* Cambridge: Cambridge University Press.

Williams, J. (1997). *Style: Ten lessons in clarity and grace* (5th ed.). New York: Longman.

Williams, J. (2002). Undergraduate second language writers in the writing center. *Journal of Basic Writing, 21*(2), 73–91.

Williams, J. (2004). Tutoring and revision: Second language writers in the writing center. *Journal of Second Language Writing, 13*, 173–201.

Williams, J. (2005). *Teaching writing in second and foreign language classrooms.* New York: McGraw Hill.

Witte, S. (1987). Pre-text and composing. *College Composition and Communication, 38*, 397–425.

Wixon, V., & Stone, P. (1977). Getting it out, getting down: Adapting Zoellner's talk-write. *English Journal, 66*, 70–73.

Wong, I. (1988). Teacher-student talk in technical writing conferences. *Written Communication, 5*, 444–460.

Wood, D., Bruner, J., & Ross, G. (1976). The role of tutoring in problem solving. *Child Psychology and Psychiatry, 17*, 89–100.

Woodall, B. (2002). Language switching: Using the L1 while writing in an L2. *Journal of Second Language Writing, 11*, 7–28.

Yuan, Y. (2003). The use of chat rooms in an ESL setting. *Computers and Composition, 20*, 194–206.

Zebroski, J. (1981). Soviet psycholinguistics: Implications for teaching of writing. In W. Frawley (Ed.), *Linguistics and literacy* (pp. 51–63). New York: Plenum.

Zebroski, J. (1994). *Thinking through theory: Vygotskian perspectives on the teaching of writing.* Portsmouth, NH: Boynton/Cook Heinemann.

Zoellner, R. (1969). Talk-write: A behavioral pedagogy for composition. *College English, 30*, 267–320.

Subject Index

Author Index